The Times Book of Best Sermons

The Times Book
of
Best Sermons

Edited and Introduced
by
Ruth Gledhill

CASSELL

Cassell
Wellington House, 125 Strand, London WC2R 0BB
215 Park Avenue South, New York, NY 10003

First published in 1995
Reprinted 1996

British Library Cataloguing-in-Publication Data
A catalogue record for this book is available from the British Library.

ISBN 0-304-33586-X

Printed in Great Britain by
Redwood Books, Trowbridge, Wiltshire

Contents

Foreword

by the Right Rev. James Jones, Bishop of Hull

I believe in preaching. But judging from modern church architecture it is a fading art. Many re-ordered church interiors do away with a pulpit, offering instead a flimsy portable contraption from which it would be difficult to give even the week's notices let alone a sermon. Lord Coggan once challenged an architect about the absence of a pulpit in a re-ordered church. The architect had raised the matter at the outset but the vicar said there was no need for a pulpit – he just speaks off the cuff.

The demise of preaching has many causes. In a culture where the average person spends eight years of their life watching television, it is felt that the sermon has passed its sell-by date. The monologue can no longer compete with the sophisticated video image, especially for the attention of the young.

The ethos of democracy has undermined the authority of any one person, regardless of being trained and ordained, to climb six feet above contradiction into a pulpit and lay it on the line for others. And yet, in spite of the cultural tide, at least one million sermons a year are preached and listened to with varying degrees of attention throughout the country.

Some theological colleges are beginning to address the fact that there has been serious neglect in teaching the art and skills of preaching. They could begin with sharing the advice that Lloyd George gave to the young Harold Macmillan after an early and poor performance in the House of Commons. 'Macmillan, that was an interesting speech of yours', the Welsh orator flattered, before deflating him. 'If you don't mind my saying so, you have no idea how to make a speech.' Macmillan was bold enough to ask the master to teach him and was rewarded with some private tuition.

'Never say more than one thing. Yours was an essay. Make one point. Wrap it up in different ways. Say to yourself as you get up: "Vary the pace and vary the pitch." Finally, don't forget the value of the "pause".' These techniques equipped Macmillan for a lifetime of oratory in both Houses of Parliament.

But although there are skills of public speaking to be acquired by the preacher, preaching is more than oratory and good story-telling.

There is a sacramental dimension to preaching. It happens within a setting of worship and like a sacrament becomes a means of communion with God. The good sermon is to be more than a reasoned exploration of the Christian faith and of the world. It is an appeal to the will to rise up and be obedient to God's rule over our lives.

One of the problems of the Alternative Service Book in the Church of England is that it drives a wedge of interminably long and diverting intercessions between the ministry of the Word and the Sacrament. How much better it would be if, after the appeal of the Word to our wills, we were able to mark our response of obedience by straightaway receiving the tokens of God's love for us. The virtue, however, of the ASB is that the sermon is placed clearly after the readings from the Bible, thus making the point that the preacher is expected not to fill the heads of his or her hearers with the latest ramblings of his or her own mind on the state of the world, but to build a bridge between the Word of God and the World of God. Too many congregations have developed the art of appearing to listen while putting their minds to work on other more engaging ideas.

Few of us preachers ever lay ourselves open to constructive criticism. Few of us dare to respond to the exit poll, 'Nice sermon, thank you' with 'Well, what in particular did you like about it?' The vicar with whom I served my curacy had the courage to issue from time to time sermon-assessment forms to leading members of the church! I remember being devastated to discover I had said 'um' forty times. I have never 'ummed' as generously again.

It is true that there are some appalling preachers who are unskilled and ill disciplined. They leave their preparation to late on a Saturday night and preach for too long. (You can always spot an unprepared sermon by the number of times the preacher says 'finally'.) One newly appointed vicar was apologizing at the door for the length of his first sermon and excusing himself on the grounds that there was no clock in the church. His seasoned Yorkshire churchwarden was unimpressed: 'Nay, Sir! But there is a calendar.'

Yet in spite of all the bad examples, many of the million sermons preached each year are faith-inspiring. I worked for seven years as an audio-visual producer and believe that modern media give us important tools for exploring the faith through video and film. But I have no doubt that there remains a primacy to preaching 'the truth through personality'. There is something uniquely engaging when a person opens the Bible and imaginatively expounds the story of God's surprising love. When it is evident that the message is already making an impact on the mind and heart of the preacher, the sermon is all the more powerful. The preacher becomes not only the medium but part of the message. The good sermon is not a cerebral exercise but involves the whole personality. As preachers open themselves to God in both the preparation and the preaching, so the Spirit and the Word shape not just the sermon but their very lives and those of the their hearers. It is at that moment that preaching can become prophetic.

Acknowledgements

Special congratulations to Alison Fry, Jeremy Davies, Richard Major, Gill Dascombe, Barry Overend and Edmund Marshall, selected from the thirty preachers whose work is published here, to compete in the final of the Preacher of the Year Award 1995.

Extract from *The Summons* by John L. Bell & Graham Maule, from the *Heaven Shall Not Wait* collection (Wild Goose Publications, 1987) © 1987 WGRG, Iona Community, Glasgow G51 3UU, Scotland, quoted in Clare Herbert's sermon and reprinted by permission. *The Example* by Hilaire Belloc from *Complete Verse* quoted in Richard Major's sermon and reprinted by permission of the Peters Fraser & Dunlop Group Ltd. *The Annunciation* by Edwin Muir, quoted in Jeremy Davies' sermon and reprinted by permission of Faber and Faber Ltd. Lyrics from *The Gunner's Dream* (Waters) © 1982 of Pink Floyd Music Publishers Ltd, quoted in David Johnson's sermon and reprinted by permission of the publishers. Quotation from Lord Hailsham *The Sparrow's Flight*, quoted in Donald Denham's sermon and reprinted by permission of HarperCollins *Publishers* Ltd. Extract from *Lord, why did you tell me to love?* by Michel Quoist from *Prayers of Life* quoted in Barry Overend's sermon and reprinted by permission of Gill & Macmillan Publishers.

Introduction

by Ruth Gledhill

Preaching has received a bad press for many years, long before the Rev. Sydney Smith said a century ago that a dean of his acquaintance deserved 'to be preached to death by wild curates'. Religious jokes often start and finish with a vicar in the pulpit, and most preachers now stand before a lectern to deliver their word, rendering them safe from the charge that they have placed themselves ten feet above criticism. Although G. K. Chesterton believed that it was the test of a good religion whether you can joke about it, many take the line today pursued by Sigmund Freud, that when a man is free of religion, he has a better chance to live a normal and wholesome life.

Five hundred years ago, Machiavelli wrote that 'there can be no surer sign of decay in a country than to see the rites of religion held in contempt'. Preaching today is widely held in just such contempt. Whether it is the fault of preaching and preachers, or of the congregations, is unclear. Certainly, the rise of scepticism since the first world war, and the steady decline in churchgoing after the second, have contributed to the malaise. The consistent abuse by dictators of their oratorical skills to shepherd masses into the evil that this century has been witness to has further discredited such skills and added to the cynicism of a reasoning public. The days when good preachers were men of influence, when one preacher, Spurgeon, had his Sunday sermons printed in the next day's newspapers, seem largely to be gone. A powerful sermon by the Archbishops of Canterbury and York, or another bishop or lesser clergy even, can attract wide publicity when critical of government or social policy. But even then the sermon will rarely be printed in full, and the condemnation heaped on the heads of such brave clerics at these times can be enough to put them off ever again ascending another pulpit.

Not surprisingly, preaching, arising out of a centuries-old tradition of prophecy and oratory, receives a good press at least in the Bible. In some versions of St Mark, we see the risen Christ stating: 'Go ye into all the world, and preach the gospel to every creature' (16:15). In his letter to the Ephesians, St Paul describes preaching as a grace (3:8). Perhaps some prize should go to the two or three *Times* readers who submitted, whether through logic or a lower form of wit, the Sermon on the Mount, by Jesus Christ, to the Preacher of the Year award.

The worst sermon I have ever heard was also the shortest. The clergyman concerned was clearly suffering a bad hangover and might have been at the bottle again that morning. He could hardly complete a sentence, evidently forgetting the beginning of it when he reached the middle, and if he did get to the end, he seemed to be completing one that he had begun a few paragraphs earlier. His sermon preparation might have been done in the car on the way to church, if indeed he had been foolish enough to risk driving in such a state. The moral I drew from his sermon was never attend that church again.

Conversely, the best sermon in my memory was the longest. Delivered by an eminent churchman, it was a clear and chilling indictment of the moral turpitude of our era. I left the service feeling profoundly changed by that man's words, bearing an unshakeable certainty that, without faith, our world faced an extremely precarious future. I would travel many miles to hear that man preach again.

Yet bizarrely, whereas in the Victorian era an average sermon would last forty-five minutes, and in the middle of this century might take twenty-five minutes, today it is rare to hear a preacher speak for more than fifteen, and woe betide him or her if he or she does. I have sat sometimes in a church on a hot summer's day where entire rows of elderly congregants have been asleep. At times I have barely resisted dozing off myself, the soft tones of the preacher's voice a welcome soporific akin to the buzzing of bees around flowers in a country garden. Good sermons are now generally considered to be short rather than long. If P.G.Wodehouse was writing *The Great Sermon Handicap* today, it is likely that the inimitable Bertie Wooster would no longer bet unsuccessfully on which country parson would preach the longest sermon in a race won by an outsider who preached another clergyman's sermon, lacking one of his own. P.G.Wodehouse might well instead have his parsons competing to be in and out of the pulpit in the shortest possible time, and the winner might be the cleric who decided not to preach any sermon at all.

Dr Martyn Lloyd-Jones of the Westminster Chapel, described as 'the last of the great preachers' until he retired in 1968, thought preaching 'the highest and the greatest and the most glorious calling to which anyone can ever be called'. Yet in the comparatively short time that has passed since, preaching has become an increasingly disparaged art. I was told once that what a preacher needed above all else was imagination – to imagine that someone was listening to what they were saying, and that it might make a reasonable difference to that individual's faith and life.

Preaching still demands some of the traditional and ancient skills of oratory and rhetoric, the ability to persuade with a combination of reason and emotion, where intellectual cool does not douse the fire, and where emotion does not sweep away intellect. But the height of preaching as an art, in the late eighteenth and early nineteenth century, coincided with the golden age of political oratory. There can be no doubt that the rise of television and radio have had a profound impact on styles and methods of preaching and persuasion, and different skills are now required. Nowadays many preachers are lost for words if they have no microphone, but the use of a microphone requires a completely different technique from the voice projection preachers have been taught.

My own experience has taught me that there are few experiences more terrifying than climbing into a pulpit to preach a sermon. All preachers, no matter how bad, deserve some degree of gratitude and praise from their public. I once accepted invitations to preach at colleges at both Oxford and Cambridge, and was left reluctant ever to try again. Arguments that seemed fine in print turned watery when uttered, and in any case could barely be spoken out loud by a mouth atop a body and legs shaking with fright. With better preparation, my most recent experience, at St Mary's, Oxford, proved slightly less humiliating, apart from the breakneck speed at which the terror incumbent to the experience propelled me to read my notes. The facility with which my heart was pierced and my concentration killed, as if by a stone, when even one member seated in that packed church evinced the slightest sign of boredom, was truly horrible. These experiences increased my understanding invaluably. Preaching sermons is unlike any other art: you are not presented with an audience, but a congregation. They might be there to be entertained in part, but generally speaking they are there because they want to come closer to God. As the preacher, it is your job to help them on that journey. Preaching is thus unlike delivering a lecture, because it demands the passion and commitment of faith. But it is also unlike standing on a soap box at Hyde Park, because it demands a respect for the intellect, problems and interests of your congregation.

This book of *The Times* best sermons arose out of a desire to help both preachers and congregations have a better time, and to convince an unbelieving public that there are still messages being spoken in the thousands of beautiful churches throughout our land that deserve to be heard. The sermons reproduced here are the thirty shortlisted by the College of Preachers from more than 500 entries to the College's Preacher of the Year award, sponsored by *The Times*. The book is being published on All Saints Day, when the six finalists in the award will take part in a service of prayer, music and worship to decide on the winner. Many preachers, being in a profession where humilty must be cultivated almost as a grace, have understandably felt reluctant to put themselves forward for such an award. But preaching cannot be sacrosanct. Like it or not, the Church and its leaders cannot set themselves above or outside the day-to-day demands and values of a market-led world, although some, of course, might argue that this is precisely what they should be doing. There can be few better examples of courage and conviction than that of the men and woman whose words are printed here, whose willingness to expose their beliefs and faith to public scrutiny is testimony that they, at least, are among those who truly do attempt to practise what they preach.

John the Baptist

Sermon preached by Alison Fry at St Michael's with St Paul's, Bath, on 11 December 1994.

Alison, 30, an ordinand in the Church of England, this year completed her degree in theology at Cranmer Hall, St John's College, Durham. She hopes to be ordained deacon next summer, and subsequently to be priested. She has preached regularly on her placements in parishes during her studies, and although it makes her nervous, she feels it is what she has to do. She has had a vocation to the ministry since her early 20s, but initially pursued a career in biochemistry. She gained her first degree at Newnham College, Cambridge, and a doctorate at Hertford College, Oxford, specializing in plant biochemistry. She hopes to be a parish priest, but has a passion for learning and is unlikely to stop studying. Dr Fry says: 'One of the reasons I am particularly keen on preaching is that I think it is one of the few forums where people are called upon to listen and use their own imaginations and participate in what is being said. We live in a culture of 30-second soundbites, where we are bombarded by visual images the whole time, and if preaching is communicating anything it is communicating a relationship with God which is a personal relationship, needing to be communicated in a personal way, by a person.'

Bible texts: Isaiah 40: 1-11; 1 Corinthians 4:1-5; John 1:19-28

This is how one should regard us, as servants of Christ and stewards of the mysteries of God.

[1 Corinthians 4:1 RSV]

If you chat to my Mum and Dad after the service, they will tell you that I have always, probably even before I could read, had my nose in a book. My favourite pastime, second only to browsing in book-shops, is to settle down with a good mystery story, or to watch one on telly. What do I find fascinating about a good mystery? What is it that makes a good mystery story? Well, it usually begins with some strange goings on – deaths in suspicious circumstances, people behaving oddly, puzzling clues. This leads to questions and intrigue as the hero or heroine sets about solving the riddle. And then the suspense mounts as we expect the plot to take a certain turn and it does not. And finally there is the solution. Sometimes we can't wait and turn to the back page for a peep; but usually half the enjoyment is to see if we, the reader, can solve the mystery, find out 'who dunnit' before the end; we all know it is going to be solved before the end of the book. There are strange goings on, questions and intrigue and all is revealed in the end.

There are some strange goings on in the Judaean desert in the first century. A man called John is behaving in a pretty odd way. He is preaching an uncomfortable message in an uncomfortable setting. He dresses in camel hair, eats locusts and preaches that people should repent and be baptized. I'm sure some people thought he was off his trolley but, as the other Gospel writers tell us, many more went to hear what he had to say. And they were convinced by it.

He caused quite a stir. It is hardly surprising then that the religious authorities had some questions to ask – were intrigued by these strange goings on – and started searching for answers. In true detective fashion they decided that the best place to start was to question the suspect. So off went the priests and Levites to the desert to ask John Baptist 'Who are you?'

Now, if I ask Alastair, 'Who are you?', the chances are he'll say something like: 'I'm Alastair Wallace, Rector of St Michael's with St Paul's, married to Judy, with three children', and so on.

If I say to Alastair 'Who are you?' and he says 'I am not Howard Latty [church warden]', I might begin to wonder if it were time for our Rector to take another sabbatical.

But look at John the Baptist. He doesn't say, 'Hi guys, I'm John the Baptist'. When the priests and Levites say 'Who are you?', he says 'I'm not the Christ'. They hadn't asked him if he was the Christ. How odd! What is he playing at? Curiouser and curiouser! More mystery, more intrigue.

In the first century there was a great expectation that the Messiah would come soon. Israel was in a mess. There had been civil wars for the preceding 100 years, the country was under Roman occupation and it was some 400 years since the last prophet had spoken. What was God up to? They were supposed to be God's chosen people. Hadn't he promised a king, a leader from the line of David, who like David, as the 'anointed one', the Messiah, would lead his people to be a great nation again? Why the delay? Why was God silent for so long? Surely the Messiah would come soon.

It would be natural to get excited about this odd character, baptizing people in the Jordan, and for some people to think that he might be the Christ, the Messiah. John knew what was in the back of their mind when he answered the question 'Who are you?' He said he was not the Christ.

But saying '*I* am not the Christ' leaves open the possibility that the Messiah is still to come, and imminently.

Another expectation at the time was that the Messiah would be preceded by a reappearance of the greatest of all prophets, Elijah. This is based on Malachi 4:5:

> Behold, I will send you Elijah the prophet before the great
> and terrible day of the Lord comes.
>
> [RSV]

You'll remember from 2 Kings 2:11 that Elijah was translated into heaven in a whirlwind and, not having died as such, he could easily have been expected to return to hail the coming of a new king, the dawn of a new age. 2 Kings 1:8 has Elijah dressed exactly as St Matthew says John the Baptist was dressed. What John the Baptist was doing, the way he was behaving, suggested that he was Elijah (Matthew 11:14 and 17:12 specifically identify him as Elijah).

It is not surprising that the priests and Levites ask: 'What then? Are you Elijah?' But again he says he is not. There goes another theory!

But saying '*I* am not Elijah' deliberately opens up the possibility that he is someone just as important. What is he playing at? More mystery, more intrigue.

Our detectives (the priests and Levites) are running out of options. The plot is not going as they expect. What else could possibly explain this man's odd behaviour? 'Are you the prophet?' they ask, expecting the fulfilment of Deuteronomy 18:15:

> The Lord your God will raise up for you a prophet like me [i.e. Moses] from among you, from your brethren – him you shall heed.
>
> [RSV]

If he is not Elijah, then at least he must be a new prophet to break God's silence. He says 'No'.

Then, by what authority is he teaching and baptizing? They ask him again 'Who are you?...What do you say about yourself?' Even now John the Baptist does not give a straight answer.

> I am the voice of one crying in the wilderness, 'Make straight the way of the Lord', as the prophet Isaiah said.
>
> [John 1:23 RSV]

He seems to be contradicting himself. Now he is saying he is the forerunner, the one who is to announce the coming of the Messiah, yet he has just said that he is neither the prophet nor Elijah. What is he playing at? The priests and Levites are getting exasperated.

> Why are you baptising if you are neither the Christ, nor Elijah, nor the prophet?
>
> [John 1:25 RSV]

The mystery continues.

> I baptise with water; but among you stands one whom you do not know, even he who comes after me, the thong of whose sandal I am not worthy to untie.
>
> [John 1:26 RSV]

What is he talking about? Are these the rantings of a madman? Or is he claiming some new authority on the basis of Scripture (Isaiah 40)? Is he saying something long expected is about to happen in an unexpected way? Is that the attraction? A mystery.

Of course we *think* we know the end of the story. We have read the rest of St John's Gospel, we may have seen the film and even have the

T-shirt. We know that John the Baptist was not the Christ, and that he left open the possibility that the Christ was to come after him. We know he was not the expected Elijah, nor the prophet. He was a new kind of messenger for a new kind of Messiah. Jesus was not the military leader everyone expected, but an itinerant preacher who died on a cross; neither was John the obvious messenger everyone was expecting (Elijah or the prophet), but an enigmatic figure who spoke in riddles. He was the one who announced the coming of Jesus.

We think we know the end of the story. We have the solution to the clues St John leaves throughout his Gospel. We know that John the Baptist was telling us about Jesus when he spoke in riddles to the priests and Levites. We know that when he referred to the Lamb of God, or the Son of God, in the next few verses, he meant Jesus. We have put the clues together and we know that the Gospel of John tells us about Jesus. He was the one who was among them yet they did not know him, he was the one whose sandal John was not worthy to untie.

Perhaps we worked it out for ourselves. Perhaps someone else explained to us who Jesus was. Either way, we think we know the end of the mystery. And it loses its cutting edge. No longer is it a mystery. The strange goings on in the Judaean desert are explained. The questions of the priests and Levites are answered. The suspense is gone – we know where the plot is going – we know Jesus is to come (that's what we celebrate at Christmas).

It's an old story and it has become familiar. Is that why the Church's message doesn't seem to attract people? Have we lost the sense of mystery that draws us compulsively to discover and explore who Jesus is (who God is) – like a good detective novel? Have we lost the curiosity that drew people in droves into the wilderness to hear John the Baptist? Have we lost the sense of expᵔctation and wonder that something new and exciting was about to happen, an expectation that drew the crowds? Have we lost the idea that something is happening that is so different and radical that it worries the religious authorities? Are the strange goings on so familiar that there is no sense of intrigue or suspense?

We have, if we think we know the end of the story. It is no longer a mystery if we think we know the end of the story. But I want to suggest that we do not.

The mystery of the man in the desert with his enigmatic answers to the priests and Levites does not end with Jesus' birth. It does not end with Jesus' teaching. Or his death, or his resurrection, or even at

Pentecost.

The end of the mystery is still being written. In you and in me. Who Jesus is, who John the Baptist was pointing to, is still being told. In you and in me.

There are some strange goings on in our society today.

'I can't believe it. He is such a good neighbour – he'd do anything for anyone.'

'It's amazing. She just radiates peace and calm.'

'Do you know, I went to the church up the road and felt really welcomed.'

'You'll never believe it but they actually give away mince pies at St Michael's.'

There are some strange goings on in our society today. Do we pass on to others an infectious sense of excitement at never being quite sure what God will do next – even in the little things of life? Does the way we act pose questions about this God of ours? Why *are* Christians like that? Do we intrigue people by the way we are? By our peace and security in the knowledge that we are loved and accepted by our heavenly Father? Do we proclaim the mystery of faith and so draw others to it – like a good detective story?

> This is how one should regard us, as servants of Christ and stewards of the mysteries of God.
>
> [1 Corinthinians 4:1 RSV]

May we be good stewards.

The Annunciation

Sermon preached by Jeremy Davies at Salisbury Cathedral on 18 December 1994.

Jeremy, 49, moved to Salisbury in 1985 after seven years as senior chaplain at Cardiff University. He was ordained deacon in 1971 after reading English and then a second degree in Theology at Corpus Christi, Cambridge. Brought up a Baptist, he wanted to be a priest for as long as he can remember. He says. 'Preaching is pivotal in building up the Christian community. Coming between the day-to-day world and the sacramental life, the sermon is trying to interpret the one to the other and making the connections.' His text was the Edwin Muir poem, 'The Annunciation'. The scriptural context was that day's Gospel reading, the story of the Annunciation in Luke's Gospel.

The angel and the girl are met.
Earth was the only meeting place.
For the embodied never yet
Travelled beyond the shore of space.
The eternal spirits in freedom go.

See, they have come together, see,
While the destroying minutes flow,
Each reflects the other's face
Till heaven in hers and earth in his
Shine steady there. He's come to her
From far beyond the farthest star,
Feathered through time. Immediacy
Of strangest strangeness is the bliss
That from their limbs all movement takes.
Yet the increasing rapture brings
So great a wonder that it makes

Each feather tremble on his wings.

Outside the window footsteps fall
Into the ordinary day
And with the sun along the wall
Pursue their unreturning way.
Sound's perpetual roundabout
Rolls its number'd octaves out
And hoarsely grinds its battered tune.

But through the endless afternoon
These neither speak nor movement make,
But stare into their deepening trance
As if their gaze would never break.

[Edwin Muir, 1887–1959]

W hat if she'd said 'no'?
What if she'd been too busy; or too conventional; or too afraid?
There were a hundred ways of getting out of it: 'It's market day', 'I'm
not that sort of girl', 'It's the wrong time of the month' .

For a fleeting moment the consequences of saying 'yes' ran past
her; the stranger saw the fear and panic in her eyes and hastened to
reassure her. 'Do not be afraid: you have found favour with God.'

Well, God's favour was one thing: an important thing I'm sure and
thank you very much; but I've got to go on living in *this* community,
with these particular neighbours, in this particular tight-knit,
traditional, hard-working peasant village. I'm not sure that saying
'yes' to you will find favour with them.

And the shape that God's favour would take? To be the mother of
God's son. The joy of every Jewish woman's heart is to be a mother:
to put off the shame of virginity or sterility and join the matriarchal
throng; responsible for the continuation and nurturing of the covenant
people of God. But what a sour joy – to be an *unmarried* mother in a
Jewish village; more degraded and ostracized than simply being an
unmarried virgin. We don't need to be daily listeners to *The Archers*,
and to the complex reactions of Shula and Cathy to motherhood, to
know that having a baby is not the favour everyone wants.

What if she'd said 'no'?

No one would have blamed her: in her position we would have

done the same. Indeed, although Christian iconography has persuaded us that this particular woman was God's only choice, it is possible that the stranger had knocked on several doors before this one, like some Dandino in the Christmas panto' seeing if the slipper, as it were, would fit. After all, God's plans had been thwarted by women and men – even highly favoured ones – saying 'no' before. Maybe, in Mary, the barrel was being scraped and God was truly exalting the humble from their low estate.

What if she'd said 'no'?

All heaven held its breath as God's mighty plan for the redemption of the world hung upon the 'yes' or the 'no' of a slip of a girl from Nazareth. That perhaps is the most remarkable thing about the whole episode: that all the divine eggs were put into one highly vulnerable basket. I suppose there might have been a contingency plan. After all, you could read the Old Testament as God's great contingency plan. Not so much the story of God's constant initiative of love and judgement in human affairs, but God reacting, trying to find another way round human intransigence; coping with our God-given capacity to say 'no'. There might have been a contingency plan, if yet again this maid, true to her human kind, had opted for convention, for safety, for obscurity. But nothing in any contingency plan could change the fact that the Almighty God had tethered himself and his good purposes once and for all to the yes or the no of the beautiful but wilful creatures he had made in his own image and likeness. Their co-operation, their participation, their freely given yes to him was a crucial and indispensable ingredient in whatever redemptive plans the great God might have. There were no short cuts: there are no short cuts. God has put himself entirely in the hands of a Jewish girl, because only from this acceptance, this God-given capacity to say 'yes', could God's original creative purpose come to fruition. Which is why Edwin Muir in his poem on the Annunciation, 'The angel and the girl are met', sees the encounter between Mary and the stranger, who is none other than God himself, as a meeting between lovers.

> See, they have come together, see,
> While the destroying minutes flow,
> Each reflects the other's face
> Till heaven in hers and earth in his
> Shine steady there. He's come to her
> From far beyond the farthest star,

Feathered through time. Immediacy
Of strangest strangeness is the bliss
That from their limbs all movement takes.
Yet the increasing rapture brings
So great a wonder that it makes
Each feather tremble on his wings.

There's a suggestion of sexual encounter in the 'increasing rapture' and the 'trembling feather', but much more than that, this is a meeting of mutual self-giving in which both the maid and the stranger are reaching out to each other in mutual esteem, both saying 'yes' to the other. As they look into each other's eyes they see not only their own faces reflected in the other, they see heaven and earth joined together. Of course this is a love poem, pure and simple, if either love or poetry could ever be so simply and purely described. But it's a love poem that sees the Gospel truth that God's disclosure of himself arises, and can only arise, within that relationship of mutuality and self-offering to another, and saying 'yes' that we call love.

What if she'd said 'no' ?

She had no choice. At one level she had all the choice in the world; she could have said 'no', or 'wait', or 'perhaps'. She saw the consequences – or some of the social consequences at least of saying 'yes'. But when the angel and the girl are met, when the moment comes, there *is* no possibility of saying 'no' for either of them.

Muir's poem continues: while this secret love-making is going on, life goes on outside the window; as though to remind us that the Annunciation did not take place in some rarefied atmosphere of sanctity, but on the main concourse, in the midst of the traffic.

Outside the window footsteps fall
Into the ordinary day
And with the sun along the wall
Pursue their unreturning way.
Sound's perpetual roundabout
Rolls its number'd octaves out
And hoarsely grinds its battered tune.

Which moves us from sacred story to ordinary day: to the places which we inhabit; where we buy our lottery tickets; where we worry about money; where we grieve and feel guilty over the relative who has had to go into a home; where we over-indulge; where we do our shameful things as well as the things that surprise us by their generosity. I'm talking about Monday morning, with Sunday and its story a half-forgotten memory. As we hurry into town the leisure of Mary's love tryst will be the very last thing on our list: turkeys, cards, wrapping paper, presents for forgotten friends who just happen to be passing on Christmas Eve. As we hear the hurdy-gurdy organ in the market square churning out comfort and joy we may press a hurried 10p into the begging hand of a wayfarer or the rattling boxes of a local charity. Over a quick cup of tea before getting the children from school we may turn on the radio and hear the point-missing syncopation of a John Rutter carol. We may even be seduced by the saccharine view of Christmas, with shepherd boys piping, and angels manger-hovering like demented midwives. But if we are persuaded by that sentimental view, then I fear what we celebrate today and what we shall be celebrating next Sunday will be little more than a fairy story. For the story of the Annunciation is not simply a two thousand-year-old fable which it pleases us to embellish and gaze at like some old master we can wonder at and turn away from. The Annunciation is the most relevant New Testament story for us today: just the other side of the window where our footsteps fall, just the other side of the ordinary day, just at the end of this road to the market square, an angel waits; God waits. The question is not: 'What if she'd said "no"?' (An idle speculation: we know she didn't). The question is: 'What if *we* say "no"?'

Or more importantly: 'What if we say "yes"?' For the Annunciation, like the sacrifice of Calvary, is something that happened once for all, and can never be repeated. And yet, annunciations like crucifixions take place every ordinary day, as God encounters us, addresses us, discloses his love to us and longs for us to answer 'yes', 'Amen', 'Be it unto me according to your word'. The consequences of saying 'yes' may run before our eyes. The excuses – the understandable excuses – will form upon our lips. But if we can get past John Rutter we may find, in the business and busyness of this week, that God, having put a wafer in our hands as a token of his presence today, is staring into our eyes tomorrow, yearning for us to say 'yes' to him and to cradle his new life with all its terrible demand, and transforming joy.

But through the endless afternoon
These neither speak nor movement make,
But stare into their deepening trance
As if their gaze would never break.

The Message of Christmas

Sermon preached by Ian Paul at All Saints' Church, Branksome Park, Dorset, on 18 December 1994.

Ian, 33, an Oxford mathematics graduate and former businessman, trained for the ordained ministry in the Church of England at St John's theological college, Nottingham, in 1989-92 but postponed ordination to study for a doctorate in hermeneutics, or biblical interpretation. He aims to complete that by next summer and then go forward for ordination as a stipendiary assistant curate in the Salisbury diocese. He is also managing editor of Grove Books, a small Christian publishing company in Cambridge. His wife, Maggie, is a GP. He preaches once or twice a month. 'It's always daunting before you start, because you have a Bible text, a congregation and nothing to say. That feeling of trepidation is always intimidating. It is very much a case of waiting on God to see what he wants me to say from the text.' On this occasion, unusually, he did not preach from a particular text but took as his starting-point the 'dream of innocence' present in human experience.

I love Christmas. I love this time of year. There is something wonderful about it all. I know that there is the danger that it will all get swallowed up in commercialism, but there is still something wonderful about it all.

There is something wonderful about lights shining out from winter windows. There is something wonderful about people being nice to total strangers for no particular reason. There is something wonderful about standing on an icy street corner, holding a soggy song-sheet with frozen fingers, belting out 'Hark the Herald' under the light of a swinging lantern. There is something wonderful about mulled wine and mince pies afterwards. There is something wonderful about the silent beauty of falling snow – the crunch of shoes and the squeak of tyres and the muffled stillness of the world once snow has come. There is definitely something wonderful about this time of year.

Why? Why do these things stir up this magical feeling inside? I think it is because it awakes in us a dream of innocence – the memory of a time when life was less sordid, less complicated, less troublesome. When we were young, it seems as though we had a lot less to worry about – no mortgage, no concern about job security, no stress, no elderly parents getting noticeably older by the year, no anxiety about our children, their education, their work, their lives and relationships. Life was a lot less complicated – I did not need a computer to organize sending my Christmas cards. We had a lot less to feel bitter about – the hurt of broken relationships, resentment about work pressures, loneliness from being stuck at home, an awareness of our own health slipping away as we get older.

And all the things of Christmas remind us of this time of innocence. And yet, it is not really a time in the past. I think we all harbour this dream of innocence; we long to rediscover it now.

There is a part of us that longs to be able to live and work with a clear conscience. There is a part of us that longs for the confidence to handle relationships with integrity. There is a part of us that longs for the moral courage to say 'no' to the injustices we see around, to make a difference, not simply to be one of the masses who carry on with the routines of life, indifferent to the sufferings of those around us. There is a part of us that longs to give ourselves to a cause, to something or someone really worthwhile, and genuinely unselfish.

We know, because we have done it once before, and we know that it felt good. It awoke once more that dream of innocence. Why does that dream fade so quickly? Why can't we make it last? Well, for one, the world we live in hates that dream, and tries to stamp it out. In our society, there are what I call 'icons of innocence' – people or things who stand for that innocence, who give us hope that there is a better way of living. But this year, perhaps more than any other, these icons of innocence have been destroyed.

We thought it was possible to live happily ever after, until the truth came out about Charles and Di. We thought that children really were innocent, until the murder of Jamie Bulger. We thought that there was a place where the poor and homeless could die with dignity, where someone really cared, until the exposé of Mother Theresa which you may have seen on television. We thought that at least some of our MPs were motivated by a desire to serve the public, until 'cash for questions' came out into the open.

One by one, our icons of innocence are being destroyed. It seems as though – to borrow some words from the Psalmist – there is no one who does what is right, not one.

We are told that we cannot trust the clergy any more, and even Santa Claus is under suspicion: as a recent television programme reported, why would an old man want children sitting on his knee? There seems to be a driving quest to 'know the truth' – or rather, to pore over the sordid details – of every fallible figurehead. Perhaps some deserve this; perhaps our illusions need to be shattered. But the result has been a widespread cynicism, and I am sure you know the definition of a cynic: someone who knows the price of everything, and the value of nothing.

We know everything we want to – except how to be different. We know we can't trust our public figures – but we don't know who we can trust any more.

But it is not just the world out there that destroys our innocence. If we are really honest, we know that we, too, are guilty of destroying our own dream. We, too, read the papers that delight in the exposé. We demand the right to know everything. We sometimes secretly gloat over someone else's downfall. And it isn't just those at a distance. We enjoy a bit of juicy gossip. When was the last time you stood up for someone else's reputation – not because you knew they were innocent, but simply because you didn't feel it right that someone should be done down without the chance to defend themselves?

We don't like to look foolish and ignorant – to be naïve about sex and money. Who wants to be the only person in the room who does not understand the dirty joke? Who wants to be the one who misses out on making a fast buck through privatization – even though we can't think it is right to make money for nothing? We would rather see someone go hungry – in Africa or in Bournemouth – than risk being taken advantage of. And if you are innocent, people will take advantage of you.

You see, it is our own selfishness and pride that destroys innocence. I remember lots of good things about Christmas, but I will never forget the Christmas I did not buy my sister a present, since she said she would not buy me one.

We would like our lives to be like that beauty of a field, or a garden, when the snow has just fallen – beautiful and clear and unspoilt. But we know that it is not long before we look more like the dirty slush that is left after only a few hours. And it is this, writ large, which we see at work in our world.

So, is there any hope? Is there an icon of innocence that will give us real hope that there is a better way to live? Is there an innocence that will stand up to the realities of adult life, that refuses to be destroyed by our cynicism? Is there someone who will show us what real innocence is, and will help us to live it out?

Christmas is the season of hope, and the message of Christmas is: yes, there is.

You see, the innocent baby Jesus, neatly tucked away in a holy manger, not complaining or crying, is actually a stained-glass illusion that we cannot believe in. Fortunately, it is not the real Jesus. The real Jesus was much tougher than that. Born of refugee parents in an occupied country, he spent his first nights in an animal's food trough. He grew up in an obscure village in a backwater of a vast empire, and almost nothing is known of his teens and twenties. He had a brief ministry as a wandering preacher. He wrote nothing. He had a small band of followers, but all deserted him when he was unjustly executed as a common criminal.

And yet, this man has affected the history of the world more than any other. What was his secret? It was that he was innocent. This innocent baby grew to become an innocent man. This was not a weak innocence, that the world despised and trampled on. He was despised, and yet he ended up changing the world. The innocent baby born at Christmas died an innocent man at Easter thirty years later. He died as he had lived, forgiving those who killed him, and not saying a word in his own defence. What a contrast to the world we live in, where we are trained to stand up for our rights, and call people to account where they have wronged us. And he died in order to give life to our dreams of innocence – or, rather, to give us a new dream of innocence. This new innocence is one for real life, not just for our dreams. Jesus wants to give us the integrity, the courage, the honesty to live right. He wants to take away our selfishness, and give us love. He wants to take away our hypocrisy, and give us openness to others. He wants to take away our bitterness and hurts, and give us peace of mind.

I love Christmas. I love all the wonderful things about it. But most of all I love the possibilities it offers. This Christmas, dream your dreams – but go one step further. Take Jesus at his word, and let him turn your dream into a reality.

Epiphany

Sermon preached by Canon John Young at St Andrew's, York (BBC Radio 4's *Morning Service*), on 8 January 1995.

Unusually, John, 58, began his sermon with an interview of a young man who lives in York and had served a term in prison before converting to Christianity. John, formerly chaplain and senior lecturer in a college of higher education, is the York diocesan evangelist, appointed by the Archbishop of York, Dr John Habgood, in 1988 to stimulate mission and evangelism throughout the diocese. John, who has written 12 books including The Case Against Christ *(Hodder), preaches every Sunday at different churches of all denominations. He says: 'One old chap told a younger preacher: "Remember there's a broken heart in every pew." Preaching is vitally important. I think it can change people's lives. It can certainly add to the quality of our lives. If there is sensitive preaching about people's lives falling apart, and they can hear in some way that gets through to them about the love of God, whatever muck life throws at people, Christian truth can sustain them. Of course, preaching must challenge us to Christian discipleship, but at the heart of preaching is the message that there is love and there is God.'*

Bible text: Matthew 2:1-12

As an introduction to the sermon I am going to interview David Greaves. David is living proof that the War of the Roses is dead, for he grew up in Lancashire and now lives in York.

[John] David, you are 24 now, tell us about your early years.

[David] Well, a sorrowful birth John. Me Mum and Dad were both very sorry. For I were a very rebellious, obnoxious young child, all the way through infant school and junior school, just doing what I wanted to do. This resulted in my being kicked out of school at the age of 11 and placed into various borstals and bad boys' schools.

At the age of 17 I left school and just wanted to get an ordinary job and be an ordinary person. But I had still a bad attitude and I got in with the wrong crowd. This resulted in serious convictions which led me to being placed in prison.

[John] A lot has happened since then. Can you pick out the key events?

[David] When I look back in retrospect, prison were a very lonely place – locked up for 23 hours a day, which gave me a desire to read. I read a book and it were about a man who had gone through a similar experience to me and one day he had this experience where God's forgiveness became real to him and from that day on he changed his life. And I read the book and thought, well if God can do that, well, hopefully, he will do it for me one day. I came out of prison and eight months later another friend of mine came and told me that he had had the same experience. God had forgiven him, so that night I just thought to myself: surely if God is real and he loves people and he can forgive, if I pray and ask him then he'll do it for me. So I prayed a simple prayer for forgiveness and as I prayed I didn't experience fireworks, but I felt a real cleanness come inside and all the guilt, shame and sin just washed away. And then a peace – and then joy, purpose and meaning put back in.

[John] How did your friends cope with the new David?

[David] Well, at first they thought I'd gone round the bend, so they laughed at me. But they soon accepted me when they realized I were very serious about what I believed in.

[John] And what about your family?

[David] Well, my family were very encouraged, because they had seen me on a crooked path and now they saw me on a more positive one, so they were encouraged. They found it a bit difficult when I were telling them about Jesus all the time though.

[John] Dave, where would you be today without the light of Christ to guide and inspire you?

[David] Well, I think I could have got my act together and lived a normal life, but realistically, I think I would have probably got deeply involved in drugs and would have been in prison more times.

[John] Thanks Dave. I'll pick that up in the sermon. But first we will sing a well-known Epiphany hymn, 'As with gladness, men of old'.

Like most vicars, I stand at the church door after a service and shake hands. I've heard dozens of different greetings. 'Thank you for a lovely service' is common. 'Nice one Vicar' slightly less so. 'I didn't agree with a word you said' is unusual but not unknown – ask the Vicar of Dibley. But the most memorable greeting came just last week. An elderly woman smiled sweetly and said, rather confidentially, 'Happy Circumcision, Vicar.' I managed to suppress a laugh as I responded cheerfully, 'A very happy New Year to you.' For it was the 1st of January – eight days after our celebration of the birth of Jesus. This special time of year is full of high days in the church calendar, including the Circumcision of Christ, which emphasizes the Jewish origins of Jesus.

My favourite winter festival fell just two days ago: Epiphany. That's when we recall the visit of those eastern kings or wise men to the infant Jesus. In the early Church, the feast of the Epiphany was even more important than Christmas itself, for it's full of meaning and significance as we see when we consider the story of the Magi.

First, they brought gifts. For some years I worked with a Spanish colleague. I gave him his Christmas present, not on the 25th of December, but on the 6th of January. For this is the custom in Spain – and in some other countries too. What better time to exchange gifts than on the day when the wise men came to Jesus with their most famous presents?

Their gifts emphasize the immense significance of Jesus. *Gold* to remind us that this baby, though born in a stable, is the Prince of Peace. *Frankincense*, often used in worship, to bring home the astonishing fact that in Jesus, God became a human being. The Apostle Paul spelt this out in his Letter to the Philippians:

He who was in the form of God, thought not equality with
God a thing to be grasped. But he emptied himself. He laid
aside his glory. He humbled himself to death. Even death
on a Cross.

It's here at Calvary that we find the significance of the third gift,
myrrh. At the very end of St John's Gospel, Nicodemus and Joseph of
Arimathea prepared Jesus' body for burial. They used aloes...and
myrrh. The shadow of the cross falls even upon the crib. So we see the
power of God revealed in symbols of weakness – in a borrowed
manger and on a wooden cross. Here we see power kept in check;
power handed over; power utterly controlled by love.

It's not for nothing that we call those ancient travellers 'wise'. For
in the gifts they brought, they showed deep insight into the special
nature of this child. History has proved them right. As R. W. Emerson
put it, the name of Jesus has not so much been written on, as
'ploughed into', the history of the world. His life split history in two:
BC...AD, the year of our Lord.

His impact continues today. The actor, Alec McGowan, set himself
the task of memorizing all 16 chapters of St Mark's Gospel – as a
hobby! To his amazement, huge audiences around the world wanted to
hear his recitation of St Mark's account of Jesus. He was asked to
reflect upon its significance. This is how he responded. 'Something
absolutely marvellous happened in Galilee, 2,000 years ago.'

The second fact about the wise men *is that they were foreigners.*
Yet the account of their hazardous journey is found only in St
Matthew's Gospel – the most *Jewish* of all the Gospels. It's as though
at the very beginning of the story, Matthew wants to emphasize that
this Jesus is not just the Messiah for the Jews, though according to
Matthew, he is that. Jesus is nothing less than the Saviour of the
whole world.

This thought is picked up by Luke in the *Nunc Dimittis.* Jesus is 'a
light to lighten the Gentiles and the glory of his people Israel'. He is a
light for all the nations.

As the wise men brought their gifts, they found a gift. God's gift.
God's gift to the world that he has made and which he longs to
redeem. God's gift to you and to me. Jesus – the Christ. The light and
hope of our world.

But gifts need to be received and accepted. And this must be done
at a personal level. In his Gospel, John picks up this theme of Jesus as

the light of the world. And he goes on: 'Yet to all who received him, he gave the right to become children of God.'

David, whom I interviewed earlier, did just that. After a rebellious life – drugs, violence, prison – he discovered and received Jesus, the light of the world. Or rather, Jesus found David – and gave light to his life.

But it isn't just wild and rebellious young men who need the light of Christ. Here in York the churches enjoy working together. And we believe that *everyone* has a story that's worth hearing. Ordinary people – and famous people too. So from time to time we invite individuals to share their experience of life and faith with us. We had a memorable visit from Lord Tonypandy – better known as George Thomas, a former Speaker of the House of Commons. And from the late Roy Castle – with Fiona his courageous wife.

The key point about these people is not that they are famous, but that they are good, upright citizens – very unlike the rebellious David. But when push comes to shove they're *just* like David. For they would tell you that their lives, too, would be dark indeed without the light of Christ. Jesus offers light to all nations. And to all members of all nations. Without exception. And that includes you and me. The Gospel is for *everyone*.

I'll end with a story – a true story – about a friend who runs an antique stall in Bermondsey. One day she bought a piece of coloured glass. It wasn't old but it was pretty and it only cost £1. Later that day she sold it for £10 and thought she'd done rather well – until later the same day it was sold for £6,000. Eventually, at auction, it raised £14,000.

The trouble was – she simply didn't recognize its worth. Perhaps it's the same for you. God's priceless gift is there for the taking – the light and hope which come from Jesus. But you don't recognize its value.

Or, maybe you're confused. So many voices point us in so many different directions. How can we be sure? You'd like to believe the Christian story but you need time to think and talk it over. If so, I'd encourage you to contact your local church – or you might write to the Christian Enquiry Agency at Inter-Church House in London.

But first I invite you to join with all of us here at St Andrew's in York as we respond to the glorious message of Epiphany – the joyful good news which assures us that Jesus is a light for all people in every age and from every culture.

[John] *Creator God,* who at the dawn of time said, 'Let there be light',

[All] Give light to our world.

[John] *Redeemer God,* whose Son gives light and hope,

[All] Shed light into our lives.

[John] *Renewing God,* whose Spirit opens our eyes to the truth of your Word,

[All] Send us out to love and serve your world.

[John only] Amen.

Lenten Sermon

Sermon preached by Christopher Fuse at St Mary's Roman Catholic Church, Loughborough, on 5 March 1995.

Ordained in 1980 after four years at the Angelicum University, Rome, Fr Christopher is a member of the Rosminian Order, a small religious order of 400 priests worldwide who are involved in teaching and parish work. Fr Christopher, who has an average Sunday turnout of 700, says: 'I was in charge of a small seminary in Rome for five years before coming here. It convinced me of the importance of preaching as a means of furthering the Gospel. It is the preacher's privilege to try and make the Gospel come alive for people who are worshipping together at that time.'

Bible text: Luke 4:1-13 [NRSV]

> Jesus, full of the Holy Spirit, returned from the Jordan and was led by the Spirit in the wilderness, where for forty days he was tempted by the devil. He ate nothing at all during those days, and when they were over, he was famished. The devil said to him, 'If you are the Son of God, command this stone to become a loaf of bread.' Jesus answered him, 'It is written, "One does not live by bread alone."' Then the devil led him up and showed him in an instant all the kingdoms of the world. And the devil said to him, 'To you I will give their glory and all this authority; for it has been given over to me, and I give it to anyone I please. If you, then, will worship me, it will all be yours.' Jesus answered him, 'It is written, "Worship the Lord your God, and serve only him."' Then the devil took him to Jerusalem, and placed him on the pinnacle of the temple, saying to him 'If you are the Son of God, throw yourself

down from here, for it is written, "He will command his angels concerning you, to protect you," and "On their hands they will bear you up, so that you will not dash your foot against a stone.'" Jesus answered him, 'It is said, "Do not put the Lord your God to the test."' When the devil had finished every test, he departed from him until an opportune time.

On the television a finger appears in the sky, it comes to point at you. You are a winner of the National Lottery. Now that's a situation that I'm sure everyone has dreamed about dealing with. What to do with all those millions? 'Of course,' we would say, 'it wouldn't change me. I'd still be careful over where I did the shopping and I'd still live in my comfortable little house and we wouldn't change the Reliant Robin for all the world.'

In a way, dreaming about pleasant temptations like winning the National Lottery is not a bad thing because it helps us realize how selfish we could be if given half the chance. Or perhaps how generous we would be...or maybe we would reflect upon how fragile is our life. How precious are our family relationships and how they could become damaged or ruined altogether by jealousies about money. Did not something similar happen to the factory worker's family in Yorkshire?

The temptations of Jesus are in the same catagory. He was offered all the world, but chose to save the integrity of his soul before God the Father.

The forty days of temptation in the desert give us this period of forty days between the beginning of Lent and Easter. We are invited to follow him and accompany him in coming closer to the Father. Let's look a little at those temptations. Let us start out on our Lenten journey in the company of Jesus and consider how his response touches our lives.

The first temptation looks harmless enough to us...'Change these stones into bread.' Now you have to be pretty hungry to look at stones and dream that they may be bread. Jesus was indeed hungry, because he had been in the desert forty days already. He was tempted to use his power for himself, and why not?

We see in his life that never did he use his power for himself. He thought always of the needs of others, and everything he did, everything he said was for others. His every conversation was for others, his acts of healing, his miracles were for others.

This is a great lesson for us. Parents do deny themselves for their children. Today, parents still work long hours of overtime, if they can get it, for their children's education. It may indeed be a more difficult decision for parents who are both in work to choose for a period not to work. They may come to realize that the children hardly ever see their parents. In that sense they would decide to go without the little extras for the sake of building up their family unity.

Thinking of ourselves is the greatest pervading temptation. It is always with us. Whose face is that in the mirror? What's in it for me? These questions should be allowed to keep coming back to us in Lent in order for us to see whether we let God into our lives. Consider that mankind lives not on bread alone but on every word that comes from the mouth of God.

Secondly, Jesus was given a vision. All the earth's kingdoms were visible. The devil would give Jesus control of these places, if he would bow down and adore Satan. The father of lies was tempting Jesus to take the easiest way out: 'Win over these people, take them, I give them to you.'

The devil pretends to have full authority over humanity. Is it like that? It may seem so at times in reading the newspaper headlines but, no, it is not so. We are God's creation and those who follow Satan must first give their will over to him. Satan says that he passes all of God's creation over to the control of Jesus, at his price.

The devil has no power that humans do not give him. Now the way that Jesus chooses to gain people for himself is to win over their hearts. In order to do that, Jesus will give everything of himself for us, even to the point of death, death on a cross. 'No one has a greater love than this, to give himself up to death for the sake of his brother.' A people given over is not a free people. Jesus insists that all who follow him will follow him freely out of love. Those who wish to follow him accept his Lordship over their lives.

This Lent we are asked to consider in what ways we may grow in freedom, how much time do we give to being joyfully with the God who made us. His is the invitation to follow him as true disciples.

Jesus did not fall for this worshipping of Satan as easily as we would have done. So Satan led him to another. The third temptation is to put on a show of throwing himself off the Temple and landing safely. In that way he would win admiration.

In walking the roads of Palestine in sweat and tiredness, Jesus was the same as all men of his time. The devil tempted him to show that he was not really human but could avoid all trouble and pain. We know how Jesus fled from those who wanted to make him king, when he made a miracle of healing for someone. We see him joyful for the good times and ready to weep at the death of his friend Lazarus. Full of energy after prayer, he was dead tired at the end of a day of work and walking. He slept exhausted on the boat during the storm. This man, though Son of God, put aside his divinity and was truly man. He was nailed to the cross and lost all his blood upon the parched earth. He teaches us that to be truly human is the greatest of gifts. To be really human is to find strength in coming in prayer to God the Father. To be really human is to share in the joys and the sorrows of others. Jesus helps us to be really human, to be serene and to be open to all.

We have forty days then to follow Jesus this Lent. In conquering temptation he dedicated himself to serve his fellow men and women. He valued liberty for all. In prayer he teaches us what it means to be really human.

It is now our turn to take up this journey of faith in which he accompanies us in order to encourage us.

The Desert

Sermon preached by Jean Simmonds at Trinity Methodist Church, Storrington, on 5 March 1995.

Jean, 49, has been a Methodist minister for three years, after serving as a Methodist local preacher for 23 years. A late ordinand, she decided to enter the ministry after working as a teacher and bringing up a family of two daughters. Besides the Storrington church, Jean, whose husband Michael works for a building society, looks after the Methodist churches at Steyning and Ashington, accounting in total for more than 300 souls. She says: 'I love preaching. I think it is vital. I love the fact that you can use preaching to relate faith to life, and that it can reach everyone. Not everyone is a reader, not everyone gets their head into a book, but a well-written sermon can reach everyone. People tell me they listen to my sermons, but it is not just what you say, it is how you say it. It is things like eye contact, the way you can bring things to life for people, open up passages they cannot understand. It is a tremendous privilege to preach.'

When I was a child, part of the joy of being taken on an outing was to stop at the shop to buy an *I Spy* book. Do you remember *I Spy* books? *I Spy at the Seaside... I Spy around London...*those little books that were meant to help us to be a little more observant and to give us some basic information. Do you remember the joy of ticking off the things you saw? There was great satisfaction in that.

I want you to come on a journey with an *I Spy* book this morning, and because it's the first Sunday in Lent, our journey will take us to the desert. The desert is a place of preparation – where God prepared the children of Israel to be his people and to inherit his promises; where Jesus was prepared for the ministry that lay ahead of him, where we begin to prepare for Easter and for all that that means in

Christian living. The Bible tells us that the children of Israel grumbled throughout the whole forty years they were in the desert. Perhaps we can understand that, because it's not exactly the ideal destination for an outing no one really wants to go there. But at some stage in our lives, probably several times over, we *will* all go there.

So what will we see? Well, the first thing that I spy in the desert is a great crowd of people. But, incredibly, each one of them thinks they're the only one. They are somehow oblivious to the footprints in the sand and to the people around them. They feel utterly alone. Who then are these people? Well, I spy Abraham, called from the security of home to goodness knows where. Sometimes perhaps it felt like an adventure, but sometimes the uncertainty of the future was frightening and made him very conscious that he was in the desert. And I spy Joseph, he is definitely in the desert. He's been taken from home, betrayed by his own brothers. He's had such wonderful dreams about what God will do for him in the future, and he's been full of hope and promise. Oh, he knows that he was insensitive in the way he shared those dreams, but suddenly God has let him down and he's in the desert. He can't understand.

I spy Moses. He's in the desert on his way to Egypt. He's afraid: God has asked him to do something that he knows he can't possibly do, it's just too much. So he's in the desert too. And I spy David. He's been anointed king, but now he is hunted by Saul as an outlaw and a fugitive. He's had to wait so long, and time and again his integrity is challenged. It's been hard, and now he's in the desert.

I spy Elijah. He's done so much: he proclaimed the truth of God from Mount Carmel. But now he's exhausted and depressed and he feels that he's got no more to give. He's in the desert. And I spy Jesus too: he's facing huge and costly decisions. And, as he struggles with them, he's in the desert. But look! Behind each of these great figures with their particular problems and concerns, I spy a long line of people stretching down through the ages, people who have shared those experiences. Some are those great people of God whose names we all know; others are ordinary folk, known well to God but to no one else. They come from all ages and cultures, all backgrounds and circumstances. Look carefully at those lines of people, trudging wearily across the desert, and, somewhere, you'll see yourself, your friends, your family, the people you know and love. They are people who've been disappointed or let down, who are hurting or feel they've failed: people who feel they are alone. Oh yes, the first thing that we spy in the desert is lots of people.

The second thing that I spy in the desert is 'testing'. I prefer that word to 'temptation' because, as our language is used today, it's a far more accurate way of describing what God does. Temptation is about leading someone into wrongdoing: testing is about proving someone's strength, revealing their worth and the gifts they've got. Here's a story which illustrates the difference between temptation and testing. There was a little boy who hung about outside the greengrocer's shop, with big eyes and a hungry expression. Eventually the greengrocer said to him, 'Are you trying to steal my apples?' 'No,' said the little boy, 'I'm trying very hard *not* to.' The desert, then, is a place of testing, and of conflict. We have to face up to ourselves and to discover our strengths and weaknesses. Our priorities will be changed.

Jesus struggled there, he fought with temptations about power, popularity and influence, about how to reveal his identity. But, at the root of all the tests which all these different people face in the desert, there is one test – or conflict – greater than any other. The fundamental conflict which Jesus faced, and which we all face, lies in the question: 'Whose kingdom are you building?' Is it your kingdom, because you care about what people think about you, or is it his Kingdom, because you know his worth? Here's a salutary exercise. Think back over the last little while and make a list of all the good deeds you've done: the way you've cared for Grandma, and the cat, and the next-door neighbour...all the things which have bolstered your feeling that you're walking God's way. Then think of all these acts of kindness as building blocks which you can use to build a tower. Now try this: each time you put a block on your tower, ask yourself the question, who did I *really* do this for? Was it because I so wanted God to be revealed in that situation? Or was it because I wanted the comfort of praise and affirmation, because I'm like a pussy cat wanting to be stroked? Did I do it for God, or did I do it for me? Work down your list and build two towers, one for God and one for you. When you've finished, which is the tallest? It's an awful challenge, and you learn some horrible things about yourself. So I spy in the desert testing and conflict – conflict over whose kingdom we're really building.

There's one last thing. I spy in the desert angels. Jesus went through everything we've been thinking about, and more. However, at the end of two of the Gospel accounts, we find the phrase: 'and angels ministered to him'. Angels...? It would be interesting to organize a

Gallup poll on angels. I'd like to devise a questionnaire. First of all it would say: 'Do you believe in angels?' If you answered 'Yes', you'd be asked to tick the description which most closely corresponded to your understanding of an angel: perhaps 'a winged being in perfect harmony with God', a 'harpist with divine powers', or a 'figure of speech used by the writers of Scripture to describe God's help and guidance'. Do you really know whether you believe in angels? It's a difficult question, and perhaps most of us don't really know what we believe...We can't deny, though, that there are some incredible stories, for which it is hard to account. What about the vicar in a country parish who was called out very late one night to a house in the most remote part of his parish where he was told someone was dying? It was a terribly dark and stormy winter's night but he got up and set off. It was a long way, and it was very dark. When he arrived at the house and knocked, there was no one there. The vicar could never make sense of it, and it troubled him for a long time. But over the years he put it to the back of his mind and eventually he forgot it completely. Many years later he was doing some hospital visiting and came to sit by the bed of a man known to be the greatest felon in the parish. The man said: 'I've got a confession to make to you. Do you remember that winter's night, years ago, when you were called out to visit a dying man right at the other end of the parish, and when you arrived there was nobody there?' 'Well yes,' said the vicar. 'I do. I remember it well.' 'It was me. I called you out. There was no one dying, but I was lying in wait for you, and I was going to kill you. But when you came you weren't alone. You had a friend with you. I couldn't believe anyone would have gone with you on a filthy night like that and I couldn't take on two of you, so I let you go.' There are questions we can't answer, and mysteries we can't define, but the Gospels state clearly that angels ministered to Jesus. In the Bible angels are often messengers, but they also, particularly in these 'desert' stories, have an important role as ministers. They ministered to Elijah in his depression and his weariness. And is not the Garden of Gethsemane another form of desert? Angels ministered to Jesus there just as they did at the time of the testing. When we find ourselves in one of those long lines of lonely people in the desert, beset by doubts and questions, in the bleakest circumstances, the deepest hurt and the most awful aloneness, we can be touched by a ministry of grace which we would never even notice outside the desert in a land of plenty. So when you find yourself in the desert, be observant and look around.

Get out your *I Spy* book and you will see that there are others who are making, or have made, the same journey. If we give the conflict to God he will use it to build his Kingdom. If we can do that we will come out of the desert with a deeper faith, a greater certainty and a stronger confidence in God. And I pray you'll experience too, in the midst of the desert, the touch of an angel – however you define an angel.

Amen.

Monkeying with the Creed

Sermon preached by Richard Major at Truro Cathedral on 12 March 1995.

Richard, a former university tutor in English literature and with a doctorate in English literature from Magdalen College, Oxford, spent a year in India teaching at a university in Delhi before he was ordained deacon last year and priest in July. He is currently Truro Cathedral's assistant curate, where his responsibilities include helping the Dean to look after the parish attached to the cathedral, as well as duties in the Cathedral itself. He has had poetry, religious meditations and academic articles published, but this is his first published sermon. He thinks preaching vital for today's world. 'We are stuck in a trivial and tongue-tied culture. There aren't many opportunities nowadays for people to hear a serious consideration of the problems of life. A sermon is one of the few remaining places where it is possible to contemplate or meditate upon, in a serious way, some of the problems of being human.'

John Henderson, an unbeliever,
Had lately lost his Joie de Vivre
From reading far too many books.
He went about with gloomy looks;
Despair inhabited his breast
And made the man a perfect pest.
   Not so his sister, Mary Lunn,
She had a whacking lot of fun!
Though unbelieving as a beast
She didn't worry in the least,
But drank as hard as she was able
And sang and danced upon the table;

And when she met her brother Jack
She used to smack him on the back
So smartly as to make him jump,
And cry 'What-ho! You've got the hump!'
A phrase which, more than any other,
Was gall and wormwood to her brother;
For, having an agnostic mind,
He was exceedingly refined.

    The Christians, a declining band,
Would point with monitory hand
To Henderson his desperation,
To Mary Lunn her dissipation,
And often mutter, 'Mark my words!
Something will happen to those birds!'

    Which came to pass: for Mary Lunn
Died suddenly, at ninety-one,
Of Psittacosis, not before
Becoming an appalling bore.
While Henderson, I'm glad to state,
Though naturally celibate,
Married an intellectual wife
Who made him lead the Higher life
And wouldn't give him any wine;
Whereby he fell in a decline,
And, at the time of writing this,
Is suffering from paralysis,
The which, we hear with no surprise,
Will shortly end in his demise.

    Moral.
The moral is (it is indeed!)
You mustn't monkey with the Creed.

                        [Hilaire Belloc, 1932]

Isn't that splendid? More to the point, isn't it true?
These lines are by the greatest of all twentieth-century Christian poets – Hilaire Belloc, who was born a Frenchman but managed very successfully to become English, even an English MP, as well as an English poet. But the great thing is that Belloc didn't anglicize his faith. He managed to carry into his poetry some of the spirit of French Christianity: exuberant, belligerent, cheerful, chivalrous, boozy,

extravagant, aggressive, colourful, moody, worldly, flowery, over-the-top.

These are characteristics of which the English Church, excellent in so many other ways, is lamentably short. But a similar exuberance was pretty typical of the mediaeval Church as a whole – including the mediaeval Church in this country. Lent, the season when we try to escape from ourselves and from our limitations, is a good time, a necessary time, to try to recover something of the mediaeval spirit of our Church, and the Continental, even the Mediterranean, essence of our religion.

We have the misfortune to live in a bleak, puritanical and severe age. And this is compounded because we Anglo-Saxons are anyway so inclined to morbid self-doubt that Lent, for us, is first of all the season of lonely defeat and self-denigration and wallowing. To remind ourselves of how rotten we are, we invent Lenten penances for ourselves which we then very carefully don't keep. It is all rather tragic and unhealthy.

Now these verses of Belloc's seem to me a good jumping-off point for this second Sunday in Lent, a good point to *stop* being too modern and too English – at least as an experiment for the next few minutes.

These verses are about faith and morality, but they approach things from an odd and alien angle, as is most desirable. They render ridiculous and satirize and poke fun at two Christian, or really sub-Christian, errors that afflict our thinking, not just about Lent, but about the whole business of good and evil, temptation and restraint, vice and virtue. And such errors are particularly rife in the English Church.

The first error is that being good wins God's favour, so that he will be nice to us, or anyway less nasty than he would have been otherwise. Being good is a way of earning good luck. Being bad invites punishment.

This is almost too silly to believe. It's a pagan or child's idea of the universe. But we humans have a genius for believing silly things, and it lurks away at the back of otherwise quite sensible minds. Consider how the

> Christians, a declining band,
> Would point with monitory hand
> And often mutter 'Mark my words!
> Something will happen to those birds!'

And of course jolly old Mary Lunn lives on into her nineties. It simply isn't true that God goes about striking people down for wickedness; indeed, as Belloc himself says in another poem:

> It isn't true!
> And if it was it wouldn't do
> For people such as me and you
> Who very nearly all day long
> Are doing something rather wrong.

If we are going to bother with goodness at all, it has to be for its own sake. There's no point in bothering just to win reward or escape punishment.

That's straightforward enough; but the second error is a bit more sophisticated, and therefore more insidious and dangerous. This is the notion that Christians, although not necessarily more *fortunate*, are nicer or better than other people.

Now it is strange that anyone should think this who has ever met a Christian. If this odd idea lurks in your mind, look around you at coffee after this morning's service. Everyone you see, including the children, and especially the choristers, will be pullulating with evil. But virtually everyone you see, also, will be drenched in godliness, for they have been incorporated into God through baptism; and most of them will just have received the most sacred thing in the world, Christ's body.

That's the oddity of the Christian situation: a situation a lot more interesting than merely struggling to fight off a few badnesses and achieve a few goodnesses over Lent. We are not trying to keep down our spiritual overdrafts, we are not punishing ourselves to prove to God we take him seriously. By acting virtuously, we are only realizing, making visible, what is already true: that we are, merely by God's action in Christ, God's children. There's nothing we can do to change that: we cannot be un-baptized any more than we can be un-born. No crime can make it less true; no heroic virtue can make it more true.

Thus the crux, the centre of Christian morality is not some fight to do more good than evil: that is a hopeless struggle. We are not to model our lives on a set of biblical rules, but obey what the Bible calls the law written in our hearts.

Or, in other words, what the Church means by goodness is ultimately a certain attitude to life and to the universe and to other people and to ourselves: *trust* in the meaningfulness of our existence; *gratitude* for our existing in the first place; *delight* in whatever we can find to enjoy in the universe, in other people, and in ourselves.

This is the attitude St Paul calls *the mind of Christ in us*. From this attitude spring love, hope and faith, kindliness, honesty and generosity, courage, sweet-temper, and hilarity – that is, finding things funny. (I didn't just make that list up, by the way, I filched it from an abbot, and you won't be surprised to hear that the abbot was mediaeval and French.) Such virtues aren't skills picked up by rote, they are living things, what Paul calls fruit. That is to say, they bloom and swell on us as grapes appear on the branches of a vine.

All sorts of people – Mary Lunn Henderson, for instance – seem to share this fundamental attitude of trust towards life; and (who knows?) their joyfulness is not so far from real belief in God, from the true 'mind of Christ', even when they don't explicitly believe in what the Church teaches.

For Christianity doesn't make you good by giving you a rule book. If we want some sort of detailed moral dictatorship, there's no point in trying to be a Christian; we'd better have a bash at joining some obscure sect. God has given us a conscience, and in the anxiety of everyday life we have to have the courage to use it, and trust in it as far as we can; and to rely on the divine mercy for the appalling scrapes which we are going to continue to get ourselves in. There is no other way: no escape from the burden and glory of being morally independent and responsible. Certainly being a Christian offers no relief from that responsibility.

But there *is* a sense in which faith is directly relevant to moral life. Those incorporated into the Church are not simply on their own. We have the example of the saints before us, the Blessed Virgin Mary first of all, and all the other saints beaming down on us from heaven, where we can only try to imagine them, and apparent in the stone and stained glass and liturgy of this cathedral, which is in that way a very mediaeval place. Moreover, we are entitled, as life members of God's sacred and universal and eternal Church, to ask for their prayers if we wish. And even if we don't, the fact remains that there is this great mystical fellowship of humanity, dead, living, and yet to be born, enduring or having endured or about to endure everything we are enduring, sometimes failing and sometimes more or less succeeding, just like us. That thought takes the edge off the lonely half-defeat of our moral lives.

But most of all, we have the Gospel, the teaching of the Church, to meditate on; or, if you like, when we come in from the clamour, tedium and chill of life, we can warm our hands on it.

Some people think or even say that doctrine doesn't matter, and that Christianity is just about leading a good life. Such people are very foolish. We are about to recite the Nicene Creed, that is, chant our way through a series of theological propositions. Why? Particularly, why the palaver about that central proposition: 'For us and for our salvation he came down from heaven...and was made man'? Some of us have the custom of bowing at those words, to concentrate the mind – but to concentrate our minds on what? Well, on the central idea of Christianity, that God and man are not separate but one. And if that central idea is true, everything about human life is transformed: including, along with everything else, the art of being a good person. Robert Runcie describes human goodness as the 'reflection of the light which shone in the face of Jesus Christ – the light of the knowledge of the glory of God. In that unquenchable light we see what human nature is called to be.' And all that Runcie is saying here is that he believes in the doctrine of the incarnation, and knows it to be morally relevant.

So:

> *The moral is (it is indeed!)*
> *You mustn't monkey with the creed.*

Monkeying with the creed does not mean what liberal theologians like the former Bishop of Durham do when they struggle with the Creed and try to understand it afresh. Even if we happen to disagree with them, they are taking Christian doctrine seriously, they are doing their job. No: it is those who say they believe every word of the Creed, and then plod through life obeying a few little rules, abstaining from a few pleasures, thinking God is going to reward them with heaven. *That* is monkeying with the Creed, that is trifling with Christian belief, that is opting out of the faith of the Church. *That* is to turn all life into one endless and pointless Lent.

And that's where this Lent meditation brings us. Lent isn't meant to be a lonely, hopeless struggle on our own against the world, the flesh and the devil. We have quite enough of that loneliness and that struggle as it is. Lent is first of all the Church's preparation for Easter, and at Easter we confront how *un*alone we are, how *un*abandoned. At Easter we shall confront again, not a past event, but a continuing fact: that we are not sad, monkey-like creatures meandering towards death, but godlike beings at one with the created world and with other people and with ourselves.

God knows it doesn't look that way. Things continue to look pretty dreadful; Good Friday afternoon can last for years; which is why Lent is given to us, as an acknowledgement of the desolation we are born to, of our horror at our own sickness. That horror is part of the overall picture. In this morning's Gospel Jesus, when he comes over the hill and sees the Holy City laid out before him, weeps with horror. It would be very exhausting for us if we were expected to celebrate in church all the time, in the face of our death and despair and evil. Lent is therefore given to us a *consolation*. Thus to mourn over ourselves is for us a relief.

But if that is part of the picture, it is only a small part. Lent is only forty days, it is guaranteed to end, and the austerities of Lent aren't the final word, the deepest truth, even now. The austerities of Lent are, if you like, just a way of setting off the glory of Easter; as this sackcloth, draped over the altar and round my neck as a stole, only sets off the undiminished splendour of *this* ceremony, *this* Eucharist, this rebirth into God, and indeed the whole inexhaustible richness of the Catholic Christian faith.

Responding to the splendour, church-goers in the Middle Ages ignored Lent on Sundays, and after Mass rejoiced and danced and drank. Their instinct of worldly rejoicing was a good one – even in Lent. Especially in Lent! For in the face of the eucharistic meal, our Lenten sadness falls away and we exclaim, Amen! *Bon appetit!*

Amen.

God in Creation

Sermon preached by Clare Herbert at Christ Church, Isle of Dogs, London, on 20 February 1994.

Clare was one of the first women to be ordained priest in the Church of England last year. She attended New College, Edinburgh, and Lincoln Theological College before being made Deaconess in 1983. She is currently Project Manager of 'Websters', a resource and spirituality centre for women in central London, and is Honorary Curate at St Paul's Church, Clapham. She has recently contributed to the book Crossing the Boundary *(Mowbray, 1994) which examines the impact of the ordination of women as priests.*

Clare was a visiting preacher at Christ Church, Isle of Dogs, and was asked to speak about her work with the Lenten theme 'God in Creation'. The hymn quoted at the end was used at the offertory and the Old Testament lesson was from Genesis 1. She says: 'The sermon is that space in the service when the Gospel is preached through the personality of the preacher. So it is a chance for Christian theology to be worked through by someone in touch with the congregation, their needs, wants and aspirations, and also their theological questions.'

Bible text: Genesis 1:31

God saw all that he had made, and indeed it was very good.

In the name of God our Creator, our Redeemer and our Sustainer. Amen.

I grew up in a place about as different from the Isle of Dogs as you can find in England. I grew up in Hatherleigh, a tiny market town on the northern edge of Dartmoor – that piece of wild windswept land covered with grey granite which forms the high centre land of the county of Devon.

Every weekend and school holiday I worked on a milk round. Some of the farms we visited on the round were on Hatherleigh Moor – a tiny patch of moorland from which you could see the wild grey hills of Dartmoor stretching in the distance. We could see all the highest Tors from there – Yes Tor, High Wilhays and beyond.

As a child I used to hate the Moor. I had a picture of it as boring, full of squelching muck, barren, lonely, a hiding-place for prisoners who would murder you or wild ponies which would stampede all over you, or so I thought. I wanted nothing much to do with it.

It's only as an adult that I've come to appreciate the Moor – England's Last Wilderness as it's sometimes called. For I made a friend who insisted I go walking there with her. In her companionship I've lain in the hot sun on the tops of the Tors, feeling the gentle breeze, listening to insects hum, beneath piles of stone weathered by 300 million years of time into fabulous piles. I've mastered rain and wind storms, learning when to turn back and why. I've ducked beneath twisted oak trees, descendants of an ancient wood. Perhaps best of all I've climbed a hill, sat and seen the sun set pink, with storm clouds gathering behind, a fabulous panoply of sky all around me, with friends, and felt the *wonder* of it.

So why, I now ask myself, was Dartmoor so closed to me as a child? I could have had a fabulous time up there. The answer comes I think that my Mum and Dad, in their old Austin A40, used to use the Moor for a quick break rather than exploring it. Most Sundays – me stuffed in the back of the car with my brother – we would *do* the Moor in the car – Okehampton, Tavistock, Princetown, Whidden Down, and home, stopping only for an ice-cream in a crowded car park or a picnic near the car. A road was never far away – even if, as on a summer's day, we shared that road with thousands of other tourists. As my brother and I got older it became a family joke –'D'you want to "do" the Moor next Sunday, Mum?'

God *saw* all that he had made and behold it was very good – God appreciated the creation, he savoured it and enjoyed it – he did not simply use it. He appreciated what was created – it was not there for him simply to use to meet his own immediate needs then to be discarded and chucked aside. God saw all that he made and it was good *in itself*. I have often asked myself since why the Moors are so empty and the car parks so full. Why are people content to miss what they miss?

It's scary to get out of the car, I think, to unlock the car door and go for a walk. The ground is often uncertain underfoot, wet or rocky – it's often uncomfortable – you have to say 'yes, I want to go for this walk' – invest in a pair of solid shoes and a friend who'll go with you.

Then, you have the shock of discovering you are different away from the car. You can go wheezy or red in the face and have to cope with going slow while everyone streams on ahead of you. You can feel a bit of a fool. *Or* you find yourself ahead of the rest, leading the way, but then you don't know how to use the map – someone gets cross with you. You find a surprising friend is good at waiting behind, while another shows off something awful. The journey starts to show you new things about yourself and others. But gradually you find it does not matter. All your faults and strengths are more obvious than when stuffed at the back of the car, but it doesn't *matter* – one is simply getting stronger and stronger, walking on the Moor.

But the greatest fear I think which stops people getting out of the car and walking on the Moor is a fear that the Moor will overwhelm us – the bog *will* swallow us up, or a storm will frighten us, or night will fall, or a mist *will* descend – because plan as we may these things *do* happen. We take a risk if we want to love and explore this world to the *full*.

God so loved the world that he gave his only-begotten Son – and what did the world *do* to that beloved Son, the great risk of the Father? It crucified him.

We are afraid the Moor will overwhelm us, and need to develop faith to face that possibility – but that faith is not developed sitting squashed in the back of the car – only fear develops there.

Learning what *stops* people getting out of the car – what it feels like to walk on the Moor and appreciate it, has helped me in my job as Pastoral Care Adviser to the Diocese of London. For every day I spend a fair bit of time listening to people who have got stuck – whether parishes stuck about where they are going, individuals stuck in how they work, or families stuck in unhappy times. And I find I often have gently to nudge people out into the wild, out into the unknown, away from the safety of how they once saw things. Often they are afraid of that exploration, wondering where it'll lead. I have to go with them, perhaps a bit like my friend walked with me on Dartmoor. And often we go to places where we never thought we would find God working and holding his creation – into broken relationships, into feelings of failure, into the darkness of depression and the wild storm of angry words. We go together into the chaos where God creates things if we walk on far enough to find them and stop long enough to appreciate them for what they are.

And I find myself helped in my faith too. For it is easy to see the Church like some sort of safe car park and God as some sort of reliable ice-cream man who should give us the sort of comfort we need as and when we want it. But whenever I treat the Church like that and God like that I get bored and sludgy, and one day wake up and wonder where my faith went.

It's when I remind myself that all the world is made by God and is to be explored and lived in him that my faith comes to life again. My faith is tested and revived by all the struggle, the beauty, the colour and the trouble of the world; it is tested and revived by all the struggle, the beauty, the colour and the trouble of being me as God made me in the world. In daring to explore the *world*, my reverence for God is renewed.

It is my hope for you this Lent that you go exploring the creation of God – that you unlock whatever door it is that *you* need to open – whether a door into the countryside, a door into somewhere in London you've never stopped to explore before, a door to prayer and silence, a door into someone else, trying to understand them for *their* point of view, a door into your own heart trying to find out what troubles you, or a door into your faith, asking what does *that* mean?

We have in Jesus the sign of God not using the world but appreciating it, living in his creation, smiling at it, crying with it. When we take the bread and wine this morning we are asked to see ourselves in Jesus, to dare to see ourselves an part of the wild risky exploration of *God himself.*

> Will you come and follow me
> If I but call your name?
> Will you go where you don't know
> And never be the same?
> Will you let my love be shown,
> Will you let my name be known,
> Will you let my life be grown,
> In you and you in me?

The Hour Has Not Yet Come

Sermon preached by Andrew McLellan at St Andrew's and St George's Church, Edinburgh on 15 January 1995.

Andrew has been a minister for 25 years and St Andrew's and St George's is his third church. He is the Convener of the Church and Nation Committee of the General Assembly of the Church of Scotland. The Committee, which deals with a wide range of social and political issues, often arouses controversy. It called this year for the lifting of sanctions against Iraq and for a new deal for people with disability. Andrew, married with children, is a frequent guest on BBC radio. 'The tradition I come from has always put a very high value on preaching and I treasure that. By no means do I think that it is only through preaching that God touches and changes people, but I do believe that through preaching God often chooses to be with us. I therefore believe that, while it is not the only thing for a minister to do, it is something that ministers must try to do absolutely as well as they can.'

Bible text: John 2:4

> My hour has not yet come.

Not yet, he said. My hour has not yet come. Not even here at Cana of Galilee where St John would later say:

> Jesus did this, the first of his signs, in Cana of Galilee, and his disciples believed in him.
>
> [NRSV]

No, my hour has not yet come. Despite the marvel of the day. Despite the sign that the tired, stale, flat religion which everyone practised and no one believed was being changed; that the thin, watery church-going which was a duty but no joy was being changed; that bubbling, sparkling spirit was on the move. Despite the fact that the water for the Jewish rites of purification gave way to the new wine of the true vine of the Gospel. No, despite the marvel of the day, my hour has not yet come.

That day, that hour, is needed and longed for yet. How easy to reduce the bubbling sparkling good news of God back to stale, weary, church-going, lifeless religion. How much the story of the changing of water into wine has to say to today's Church, and to St Andrew's and St George's and to those who make promises today. How easy it is for Pentecostalists and Charismatics and Toronto Blessing people to sneer at the cold, dead hand of established, conventional religion. How much we need the flowing, abundant life of the Gospel. But even then, my hour has not yet come. This is not it.

Not yet; despite the effect it had. Even though it was there, according to the Fourth Gospel, that the disciples believed him. Was this not the purpose of the whole adventure of destiny? Yet it was not there. It was not then. My hour has not yet come.

There was talk of 'an hour' with a woman at a well:

> The hour is coming and is now here when worshippers will worship the Father in spirit and in truth.

But even then is not his hour. Even that hour, with its vision of the all-embracing Kingdom of God, with its vision of the Kingdom of God in which women and men share together as liberated equals; even then 'my hour has not yet come'. Even that hour at the well, with its glorious hope of the friends and followers of God from different backgrounds and different traditions, Samaritans and Jews, those who call each other heretics and separated ones, those who cannot share bread and wine together, yes perhaps even with a world-embracing vision of a Kingdom of God in which those of many faiths and many religions stream from north and south and east and west and are welcomed to the great heavenly banquet of God. Even then, no, my hour is not yet come. Heaven knows how much that hour presses upon us, with fear and prejudice and bigotry on every hand. Heaven knows how important it is next week, in the Week of Prayer for Christian Unity, for us to share – if only partially and timidly – in worship with other kinds of Christians. Yet even that hour coming in a conversation between Jesus and a Samaritan woman at a well, even that hour which is coming and is now here, even then, my hour is not yet come.

When it came, it was a simple moment. A simple moment when it came. But the hour came. Some Greeks had come to two friends and said they wanted to see Jesus. And then – listen –

> The hour has come. The hour has come for the Son of Man
> to be glorified. Very truly, I tell you, unless a grain of
> wheat falls into the earth and dies, it remains just a single
> grain; but if it dies, it bears much fruit.
>
> [NRSV]

The hour is come. Some seekers after the truth would like to know more, would like to see for themselves. And at last the hour is come. Do you think that is an accident? Do you think that is an accident on this Sunday when seven come for confirmation?

Do you think it is an accident that the hour is come and the language is of death? 'The hour has come – if a grain of wheat falls into the earth and dies, it bears much fruit.' The hour has come and his hour is death. This is the hour of glory and the chimes of death are pealing and it is time for the construction of the cross. Glory, the true glory, the hour when glory is revealed, is the lifting of a broken body on a tree.

Now, the hour has come. So a towel is taken and feet are washed. How can those who follow share? How does the hour of glory become the hour for all? So a towel is taken and those who watch and those who listen know that the way to share in that queer glory is in humiliating self-forgetting service. The story of the washing of the feet begins: 'Jesus knew that his hour had come'. This is the hour to which the story moves. And this is the hour when the smelly, dirty, embarrassing pain of the world is thrust under our noses and if there is no towel in our hands we may miss our destiny. This hour had come when I walked into the home of a frightened, confused and incontinent old woman and found an elder of the Church of Scotland with towel and basin wiping excrement from her legs. The hour had come when this week's notices call us yet again to the mighty struggle which is Christian Aid in St Andrew's and St George's; when the people of Rwanda and East Timor and the judgement of God call us to pick up the towel offered to us and wash the world's poor to health. The hour has come.

But even that hour is not the fulfilment. The hour which begins with the sign of God's glory in the washing of the feet, that hour comes in all its depth and destiny, in all its pain and hope, when Jesus is taken out and crucified. And it is that hour, that hour which gives shape to the love of God, which is our hour today. Then, then, well might the words be: 'My hour has come.' What was heard was: 'Forgive them, they know not what they do.' Then the whisper might well have been, 'My hour has come', and so it was; but the words used to say it were 'Father, into your hands I commit my Spirit.' The shout might have been 'My hour has come', and so it was; though it sounded like 'It is finished.'

It is heart-stoppingly wonderful that you have come to this hour. But it is unimaginably more wonderful that this hour should have come for you. The hour has come for the Son of Man to be glorified. This day in St Andrew's and St George's Church, the hour has come for the glory of God to be revealed. That same hour of breathless love on a cross is the hour now when God loves you, loves you by name and folds you into the story, folds you into this strange glory. The hour has come for the Son of Man to be glorified. Very truly I tell you, unless a grain of wheat falls into the earth and dies, it remains just a single grain; but if it dies, it bears much fruit.

Today, that fruit can be named. That fruit is those seven whose confirmation service this is. The harvest of death and glory, is Fiona and Calum and Marjorie and Susie and Shirley and Beverley and Lynne, the people in whose confirmation service we share today.

Easter

Sermon preached by Rev. Lawrence Adam at All Saints Church, Habergam, Lancashire, on 23 April 1995.

Lawrence, formerly of Whalley Abbey where he ran the Blackburn diocesan video unit, is now Chairman and Producer of Gatehouse Television Ltd, producing expensive but quality training packages, the latest one being 'Personnel Harassment'. They are about to set up their own international publishing company. Lawrie, 57, formerly a musician, comedian and theatre producer, was ordained in 1983 after the conversion experience described below. 'A church on Sunday is the shop window of the Church,' he says. 'Some would say the sacraments are the high point, some would say the Bible readings, and I wouldn't disagree. But I would lay great importance on the sermon because, if done properly, a fusion takes place. I commit to God before I walk into the pulpit, and as I walk up the steps I am aware that my facts must be correct, that I must entertain in order to grab, that privilege has been laid on me. Above all, I am aware that people want to hear Jesus Christ and not me.'

Some years ago on a sunny day, such as this, I was standing in a crowded little ballroom in an hotel on Douglas sea-front, Isle of Man.

There was a smartly dressed member of management on a stage, and his expressionless voice was calling out names. I heard mine. 'Here,' I replied. Sometimes there would be no reply...only a silence...followed by some stifled sobs, or the sudden scrape of a chair as someone fainted against it. Friends offering words of comfort could be heard.

We were in a state of shock...it was hard to realize that only a short time ago we were presenting entertainment to happy holiday-makers, in one of the foremost and new leisure centres in Europe. It was glazed mainly with tinted Oroglass [a plastic glass] which meant that no matter what the weather was like outside, it was always like summer inside. That's probably why they named it...*Summerland.*

I had the job of presenting the main show in the Solarium, sometimes to an audience of five thousand people. I must admit that I didn't get as much pleasure out of this summer season as I normally would, I seemed to be always at variance with the management. I didn't have much faith in them.

However, the holiday crowds certainly had faith in the whole enterprise, as they absolutely flocked through the turnstiles. The publicity was certainly convincing, portraying Summerland as a safe place to bring the family! Turn the kids loose, there is no traffic here, no danger in Summerland. The place is fire-proof, they said. Exit doors everywhere.

On August the 2nd 1973, just as I was about to present a little warm-up show before the big show, the building suddenly exploded into a blazing inferno. The Oroglass melted very quickly into balls of melting burning plastic cascading down upon the crowds below. Within seconds I was in the middle of a full-scale disaster. The panicking people were hampered because of locked exit doors.

It was a miracle that only 50 people lost their lives that day. The building was burned out completely within eight panic-filled minutes! My family and myself were amongst the lucky ones. All I lost was my equipment and the remainder of a summer season.

Eventually we came out of the ballroom into the bright sunlight to the noises of helicopters hovering like vultures above the blackened shell of what had been Summerland.

The people were very quiet as they walked about the town. An eerie silence had descended upon Douglas. As I looked into the faces that walked past me, I could tell that some of them were still living with the awful memory of the night before. For many of them that would be the day that they would never forget for the rest of their lives.

The day their world came to a full stop. It would be the end of life as they had known it. They were in a deep state of extreme shock. Many of them would be numbed by the loss of their family leader, or some loved one. Never again would they see their face or hear their voice.

And if my words have made you feel sad this morning, then perhaps now you are ready to enter into the deep gloom and despair felt by people who have just experienced a disaster.

Now perhaps you feel some of the sadness the followers of our Lord felt. They would still be living with the awful memory of Good Friday: that would be the day *their* world came to a full stop. For them it would be the end of life as *they* had known it. *They* would be in a deep state of shock...numbed by the loss of *their* beloved leader. They would feel sure that never again would they see his loving face, or hear his peaceful voice. Of that they would be dead certain.

If you can somehow enter into this deep gloom and despair that they felt then I feel sure that you will be able to catch something of their sense of absolute surprise, bewilderment and fear when they looked into the tomb...and found it empty!

The fact that Mary said 'They have taken away my Lord' indicates that she thought of him as 'a dead man'. What was dead in fact was her idea of Jesus, though she didn't realize it. The bottom had fallen out of her life, and she was trying very painfully to adjust to the death of her Lord. Now, another blow had befallen her, the body she had come to embalm was missing.

Standing outside the tomb, weeping and wondering what to do, she looked in and was questioned by the two angels. In her reply she repeated what she had said earlier. With her eyes swollen from much crying she failed to recognize a third person standing near. It was his voice, rather than his face, that gave him away. Jesus had a very special way of addressing her. So she was reunited and nobody had taken away her Lord. Her hope was that now they could resume their relationship as it was before.

She tried to grab hold of him as if there had only been an unfortunate interruption, and they could return to the good old days. Oh! how often those of you here today who have suffered bereavement would want to do that.

But our Lord had to redirect her devotion that was pointing the wrong way. The Easter story is not about going back, but of going into a new relationship with Christ. Jesus had to ask her to let him go...to relax her grip. She had to learn that the resurrection doesn't mean that he had come to life again, like Lazarus. If he had then he would be subject to death again and that would be of no help to anyone. No victory. Ordinary people don't rise from the dead, but then he was no ordinary person. He overcame death, the thing that is called the 'Last Enemy'. It was a victory over hatred and trickery, and all the human weakness and wickedness that combine to put him to death. It was resurrection, not resuscitation.

The change in his body points forward to the change in our body and natures, the overcoming of all that is at enmity with God.

Mary could say 'I have seen the Lord'. This was certainly not wishful thinking or hallucination. The truth is that he had risen, transformed her and the disciples, and he can do the same for us. We must think of Jesus as somebody who not only lived in Palestine two thousand years ago, but is alive now. By faith we can say 'I have seen the Lord and know him'.

In 1976 I returned to the Isle of Man and, when I least expected it, I had a confrontation with our Lord Jesus Christ. He told me that he had chosen me, and that I had not chosen him.

I died to my 'then' way of life. A non-Christian became a believer. He said: 'Follow me.' I have followed him ever since.

And I tell you this my friends, never before have I known such peace, such overwhelming love and strength. Oh yes, I can stand up here. I can place my hand on my heart. I can personally guarantee you, JESUS LIVES.

Remembrance

Sermon preached by David Johnson at Holy Trinity Parish Church, Horfield, Bristol, on 13 November 1994.

David, 28, formerly a software engineer and recently married, was ordained deacon last year and priested in July this year, after a career as a computer systems consultant with the engineering company GKN. He sought ordination after contemplating where life might have otherwise gone, regarding it as a means of 'giving back', a response in gratitude to the love given him by parents and God. He describes preaching as 'a chance for me to draw things together. It brings together my own life and experiences, things I have done that week and things happening in the world for all of us. It helps a sense of acknowledging that God is in our lives. We have to work to recognize that. Software engineering is also a discipline of understanding, taking systems apart and putting them back together. In my faith, things have to be rational. I try to see theology as a discipline where rationality can be brought into play.'

Bible text: Matthew 5:9

> Blessed are the peacemakers: they shall be called children of God.

Remembrance Sunday has always been for me one of the most difficult days of the year. When I was a teenager I, along with most of the regular congregation, used to try and miss the Remembrance Day service at church. Unfortunately, more often than not, I would forget not to go and end up staying for the service squeezed into a side pew. It was always the hardest service of the year for me. The church was completely taken over by the civic dignitaries and members of every armed force. The whole place was full of people who were – literally – marched into church because they were expected to be there, and full of people giving the impression that they were there because Remembrance Sunday was another civic function.

Not knowing how to read in church, one of the soldiers and then the Mayor would stumble through the readings making them sound like a military handbook or an election speech. Then would come the sermon and some military chaplain or other would give a rousing speech saying how jolly good our forces were and how good they were to have won. The whole thing had a great air of self-congratulation. 'The only thing that matters in war is that we win' seemed to be the message. I used to go home angry, almost in tears. That surely wasn't what Remembrance Day should be about.

And now, a few years later, I find myself standing in a pulpit and it's my turn to say something about remembrance. I suddenly feel very humbled by having this chance to speak on such an important day for myself, for all of us here, and an important day in the life of our whole nation.

The temptation for many people since the 1960s has been to utterly condemn war. They seem to say that there is no reason or justification for ever going to war and all those that fight in wars are wrong, whatever side they are on. War, some seem to say, is something to be stopped at every cost and by any means. They say: 'War is wrong. Those who fight are wrong.' Surely that sounds like what the Christian argument should be?

But then one starts to think about that argument and one realizes just how arrogant it sounds. How presumptuous of us, who were born into a peaceful world that has been saved and re-created for us, to criticize those who fought for us. What right have we to criticize them since we know no other world than the world they gave us? These recent years seem to be times in which words are easily offered and judgements are even easier to make. And sometimes I feel as if we are becoming a generation of words and not a generation of works.

Many things come too easily to us. It feels as though we so often lose respect for the true value of many things because we do not have to work for them. We have become consumers and not producers. 'Blessed are those who hunger and thirst or are persecuted for righteousness; blessed are those who make peace,' said Jesus. Peace is something which has to be worked for and those that have worked for something know and respect its true value. The opinions of those of us who are merely consumers of that peace must, I fear, take second place.

There are only a few people here who have been actively engaged in fighting for the peace which we now all enjoy and take for granted. But I do not believe that those who fought on our behalf did so just in order to win a victory that we could celebrate. Those who fought for us believed that they were serving their country and their God and were fighting to restore peace for their world and for all those – the rest of us here today – who would come after them. On Remembrance Sunday I hope that we are not celebrating their victory in battle. We are thanking them for their service, we are remembering their colleagues who did not return from war and we are giving thanks to God for the restoration of peace to our world that was achieved through their service.

Not many things in this life come without anyone working for them. And certainly peace does not come without much work, without many people working for it, working together for it, even fighting and dying for it. That is why it is important to remember Jesus' words when he says that the peacemakers are indeed to be called the children of God. Jesus himself was a child of God – the Son of God – and he came to give his world the gift of peace and to show a way to reunite all creation with its Creator in peace. Jesus worked and suffered and died to bring that peace and those who have followed his example are truly children of God.

As Christians we spend a great deal of time talking about peace as if peace were the ultimate end in itself. But there are so many places in the world in which there is peace but where there is not unity with God. When we make our intercessions to God we so often pray for all the places where there is not peace: places in the world, situations in the world, people in the world. And peace is not just the cessation of war and conflict. Peace means more than this: peace means justice and freedom and dignity.

Even in our own peaceful country we cannot say that everyone is living in a peaceful relationship with their neighbours and their God. This country has peace but within this country suffering continues and people do not have peace in their lives. There is still work to be done and a fight to be fought. Peace is not the end of the fight. In the Letter of James is a single verse which shows that there is still work to be done. 'The peace sown by peacemakers', he writes, 'brings a harvest of justice.' We may have 'peace for our time', to quote Mr

Chamberlain, but we do not have justice for our time. There are still those who suffer in our peaceful country, those who are poor and not supported, those who are ill and uncared for, those who are homeless, those who are abused, those who live in fear. For these and for many more people there is not peace for our time.

The peacemakers whom we remember today fought for the world and for all those who would come after them. Many of those who fought for us, who are now afraid to go on to the streets at night or fear for their safety even in their own homes, must wonder what happened to the peace that they fought for. None of us can rest secure even in this peaceful country. As Christians we have a duty to carry on a fight for justice so that our world becomes a place free from fear of violence and crime and a place of justice in which all can live in dignity. If peace is to mean anything then it must mean a world in which everyone is reunited with each other and with their Creator.

And perhaps, if you would allow me, I would like to read a short verse from a song, 'The Gunner's Dream', from *The Final Cut* by the group Pink Floyd written only ten years ago following the Falklands War and the Hyde Park Bombing by the IRA. They are words that I used to listen to when I couldn't face going to church on Remembrance Sunday. I, along with everyone under the age of fifty, have no world wars to remember. But there is still a vision of peace and justice which we are reminded must be worked towards. The words describe a simple vision for the world in the mind of an airforce officer as he parachutes to the ground:

> a place to stay
> enough to eat
> somewhere old heroes shuffle safely down the street
> where you can speak out loud
> about your doubts and fears
> and what's more no one ever disappears
> you never hear their standard issue kicking in your door
> you can relax on both sides of the tracks
> and maniacs don't blow holes in bandsmen by remote control
> and everyone has recourse to the law
> and no one kills the children anymore

We are here this morning to thank and remember the peacemakers who fought to sow the seeds of peace for our time. But as we read in

James, the work has to continue: the peace sown by the peacemakers must become a harvest of justice.

We have so much to thank God for this year. We have the beginnings of peace in South Africa, the Middle East and Northern Ireland. But peace is a process and the working through of processes takes a long time. In all of these places and within our own country there is still so much to do.

When we come here on Remembrance Day there is so little that one can say and so many reminders of what there is still to do. It is not a time to express opinions or to make judgements. Two world wars happened and we live in the peace that those wars restored. We must never forget those or any wars, because by remembering them we all remind ourselves that they must never happen again. Today is not the day for words of celebration or words of condemnation. Today is a day for remembering, a day of strengthening our resolve to work for peace and justice, and a day for silence.

Evensong

Sermon preached by Peter Stainsby at St John the Baptist, Westbourne, West Sussex, on 18 December 1994.

Peter is married and has two adult daughters. He is a retired solicitor and now lives in Westbourne, where he enjoys preaching in the Parish Church three or four times a month. He has been a Reader in the Church of England for thirty-eight years. He likes a sermon to contain not only some teaching of the Christain faith, but also an application of that faith to daily life. Recently he has taken to composing his sermons on a word processor, a medium which, to his suprise, he finds more flexible than pen and ink. One of his sermons has been published in the twice-yearly Fellowship Paper of the College of Preachers.

Bible text: Luke 1:46-55: The Magnificat

If, after the first lesson, the Rector had announced 'We shall now sing "The Red Flag"', hands would have been held up in horror, letters would have been drafted to the bishop, and men in white coats would have been asked to attend at the Rectory as a matter of urgency. Instead, he invited us to sing the Magnificat: and we sang it with all the sedateness that we might have brought to the singing of 'Baa baa black sheep'. No one turned a hair. Was it because we sang to a cosy little Anglican chant – or because the English words are 450 years old and haven't quite got the bite of modern slang?

But look at it for a moment. It's a song of revolution. If we are not prepared to join the revolution, we'd better keep our mouths shut next time the Magnificat is on the agenda, we'd better keep silent when we attend Evensong. Consider some of the words (and I am quoting now from the Good News Bible).

My heart praises the Lord...he has scattered the proud
with all their plans...He has brought down mighty kings
from their thrones and lifted up the lowly...he has filled
the hungry with good things, and sent the rich away with
empty hands.

Those are not the sort of sentiments that the mighty ones, by
worldly standards, would care to hear. But they echo what the
prophets of Old Testament times were saying centuries before the date
of the Magnificat – we only have to dip into Amos or Hosea or Isaiah
or Micah to see that. They are underlining the prevalence of great
luxury on the one hand, and great poverty and oppression on the
other. Justice was hard to come by and could often be obtained only by
bribing the judge. Corruption was rife. Greed was the guiding
influence.

If we look at our own country, if we look at almost any other
country in the world today, things have not changed a lot, have they?
There is still enormous inequality between rich and poor, still sleaze
and injustice, still vast wealth in the hands of the few, whereas on the
other hand there is the most abject poverty – hunger, homelessness,
insecurity, endemic disease. We could eliminate that poverty, and all
the evils that go with it, if we had the will.

Maybe we are all guilty. Maybe we all feel a sense of shame when
we sit in our warm and comfortable homes, when at the flick of a
switch we watch the horrors in Ethiopia or Bosnia or Rwanda, or
when we are reminded of cardboard cities, here in Britain and around
the world. What had Isaiah to say about this?

The Lord will judge the poor with justice and defend the
humble in the land with equity; his mouth shall be a rod to
strike down the ruthless, and with a word he shall slay the
wicked.

[Isaiah 11:4 NEB]

The words of the Magnificat do more than simply condemn
corruption and social inequality. They provide a vision of how things
ought to be if God's plan for mankind were put into effect.

St Paul had something to say about this. Look at what he wrote to
the Christians in Corinth:

> God chose what the world considers nonsense in order to
> shame the wise. He chose what the world despises in order
> to shame what the world thinks is important.
>
> [1 Corinthians 1:27]

Time and again, the things that God did seemed to be topsy-turvy things. He chose a young unmarried girl – maybe a humble teenager – as the mother of his Son. The outhouse of a pub became a maternity ward. The family lived in a dubious town like Nazareth – Nazareth of all places. You may remember what Nathanael said: 'Can anything good come out of Nazareth?' But a little while later, when Nathanael actually saw Jesus, he was to say: 'You are the Son of God: you are the King of Israel' [John 1:49].

And the man from Nazareth, the man who was the Son of God, became a person of no fixed abode. What did he say of himself? 'The Son of Man has nowhere to lay his head.' And you recall what St John said: 'He came to his own, and his own received him not.' He was branded as a blasphemer – what irony is there – and killed like an ordinary common criminal.

The world as God wants it to be *is* a topsy-turvy world, by our human standards. In God's ideal world there is no violence, no jostling for position, no lust for power, no taking advantage of the weakness of another. Look at Isaiah again, chapter 11:

> The wolf will live with the sheep, the cow and the bear will
> be friends, the lion will become a vegetarian, children will
> play in a viper's nest.

Isaiah goes on to say, 'A little child shall lead them.' That little child is our Blessed Lord and Saviour Jesus Christ.

Today there are occasional signs of hope. Nelson Mandela shakes hands with de Klerk. Yasser Arafat shakes hands with Rabin. The British Government begins talks with Sinn Fein. The calf and the young lion grow up together. Thank God for those signs, and pray God they may bear rich fruit. But still, for most of the time, we are what we think is the right way up when God wants us to be, as it were, upside down. Do you remember what they said about the early Christians in Thessalonica? It's in Acts 17: 'These men have turned the world upside down.' Until we turn ourselves upside down, until we start a revolution, beginning in our own hearts and minds, we shall not be effective followers of Jesus. What worries me is this. I'm not sure whether I, or any of us here, have the courage for that, the courage to take our crazy religion seriously, to turn, to revolve, to be revolutionaries for Christ.

That was the vision of Our Lady of the Magnificat. That was the vision of Jesus Christ. Can it be our vision too?

One last thing. When we say the Lord's prayer, when we say: 'Thy kingdom come, thy will be done,' what do we think we mean? *What do we really think we mean?* And could we face the consequences if our prayer were to be answered?

Memorial Service

Sermons preached by John Wheatley Price at Great Bardfield Parish Church, Essex, on 5 August 1994, and at St George's Church, Preshute, Wiltshire, on 15 September 1994.

Canon John Wheatley Price is the Vicar of Matlock Bath and Cromford, Derbyshire, and preached the following sermon at the funeral of Rupert Muir and the second sermon on the death of his 94-year-old mother, Con, who was married to his father for 67 years.

Rupert Muir was the only and long-awaited child of Rachel and Brian Muir. Tragically, he died before birth in July last year. John Wheatley Price is Mrs Muir's uncle and had married the couple. John said: 'We have to try and help people from where they are. In both these services, we were able to share what faith in Jesus means, even in times of great sadness. My own ministry suggests that it is often at a time of bereavement that I am able to draw alongside people with the Christian message, which doesn't stop at death, but speaks of life, death and resurrection.' The two sermons are brief and it was decided to publish both.

Sermon to commemorate the death of Rupert William Muir, a baby.

May I begin by saying 'thank you' to Michael, your vicar, for so graciously letting me take part in this service? And to Rachel and Brian for giving me the awesome privilege of leading you all in this time of sorrow? A time which we all had hoped and prayed would have been a time of rejoicing together.

There is probably no one in church today who has not wept with Rachel, Brian and little Rupert. I doubt if any of us will get through today without tears. I know our culture says that grown men don't weep, but the Bible tells us that Jesus wept. He shared the sorrow of his friends.

I wonder how you felt? Shattered, hurt, angry, bewildered, drained, helpless? We ask ourselves 'What can I say? What can I do?' You will allow me an older pastor's privilege, as I offer some thoughts which may help friends in the village, and beyond.

Please do not think that you should not mention Rupert's name after today. We shall have many times when we want and need to talk of him. Never avoid Rachel or Brian because you do not know what to say to them – that would be cowardly! Tell them that you don't know what to say, but that you think and pray for them. A smile, a handshake, a hug can say so much.

Christmas will not be easy, but your cards will mean so much more if they have a personal, loving note rather than just your names on them. And write in your 1995 diary the date that is written in their hearts, so that you can send a token of your love to them on Rupert's day.

Some may have wanted to react like Job's wife. In their family disaster and grief, she said to Job, 'Curse God, and die.' The temptation to anger and bitterness can come very easily, especially if belief in God is little more than a kind of insurance policy against hurt. But to walk with Jesus Christ, and trust in him as Saviour and Lord is much more real, deeper and more lasting than that.

We have sung of Jesus as the loving shepherd. The Bible gives us this picture many times. Isaiah 40:11 tells us:

He tends his flock like a shepherd: He gathers the lambs in his arms and carries them close to his heart; he gently leads those that have young.

Psalm 23 begins: 'The Lord is my shepherd', not the Lord is like a shepherd, but the Lord is *my* shepherd, a statement of trust, and Jesus himself said: 'I am the good shepherd' (John 10).

The Eastern shepherd was with his flock day and night. He knew and called every sheep by name. He did not drive them in English fashion from behind, with dogs on the flanks. No, he led the way, he chose the path, he searched for the lost, he would lay down his life for them.

I shall never forget coming from Galilee, down the Jordan valley towards the close of the day. I saw some shepherds leading their flocks home. You could not have walked between one sheep and another, or between the shepherd and his sheep. They were very close, they knew his voice, they trusted him.

The picture is so vivid that a child can understand. And if you were to challenge me to prove that it is real, I would have to take you back 27 years and to Uganda. With my wife in hospital, family 4,000 miles away, but with Christian friends around me, I stood at a tiny gave, and took the service for our eldest son Andrew, who had lived but a few hours.

And if the children here ask, as children might, 'Who will play with little Rupert?', we can tell them that he is safe in the arms of Jesus. And they might find comfort too, in a way they can understand, that a member of the family was already there to love and welcome him.

May I give you one more picture before we pray? Luke tells us of two disciples walking home to Emmaus on Easter Day. They were desperately sad, hurt and bewildered. They had hoped for such wonderful things for the future, but their hopes were dashed. Jesus drew near, listened to their words, and led them to a deeper understanding of himself. Do you remember how they recognized Jesus? It was in the breaking of the bread, the symbol of his broken body, of his suffering, of his great love.

Memorial Service

Sermon to commemorate the life and death of Con Wheatley Price

Bible text: Psalm 103

> Bless the Lord, O my soul; and all that is within me, bless
> his holy name.

That is my father's favourite psalm, one of those that we read with
Mum in Savernake hospital, where she was lovingly cared for in
her last days, a psalm that expresses the Christian faith so beautifully.

For today is a *day of thanksgiving*.

Thanksgiving for a life full of years, full of faith, full of warmth,
generosity and love, of smiles and care for others. Thanksgiving for a
wonderful wife, mother, mother-in-law, grandmother, great-grand-
mother, friend.

We all have our special memories. As a family we shall share some
of these later. I remember a home where teenagers would gather on a
Sunday night, or young wives, or older ladies, or midweek groups to
enjoy life together, to learn about the Jesus the Saviour.

I remember a mother who collected bachelor curates, not to marry
them off (!) but to feed and spoil them a little. One is here today.
Many worked in the slums of Sheffield. One is now a retired bishop.
All were made to feel welcome and at home.

We remember the strict instruction given before her eightieth
birthday not to send telegrams of congratulation. 'I don't want the
village to think I am getting old,' she said. And she had a very strong
dislike of hearing aids!

I remember a lovely Christian lady, intensely loyal to and proud of
and, even in those recent months of declining health and memory,
wanting to know all about the children, their spouses, the
grandchildren and their spouses and the great grandchildren. And
when the call of God took a son to Africa and later a grandson to
South America, knowing she and Dad would only see them and their
children every three years or more, she prayed and loved and accepted
the cost for Jesus' sake.

A *day of thanksgiving* above all for her faith. Her assurance of sins
forgiven was echoed in our psalm today:

> Bless the Lord, O my soul, and forget not all his benefits:
> who forgiveth all thine iniquities; who healeth all thy

diseases...For as the heaven is high above the earth, so great is his mercy toward them that fear him. As far as the east is from the west, so far hath he removed our transgressions from us.

[Psalm 103:2, 3, 11, 12 AV]

You cannot put them further away than infinity.

It was as a girl of twelve that she came to trust in Jesus as her Saviour. That touches my heart, for I was a boy of twelve when I gave my life to him. It was Isaiah 53, read to her by her headmistress, which spoke to her heart of the Saviour's love, and the cost to him of our salvation. It was that passage that led her to a living faith in the living God. I do not know how many people she led to Christ, but I do know it included my father.

Last Thursday afternoon at her bedside, before Jean and I had to return to Derbyshire, I read these words that Paul, near the end of his life, wrote to Timothy:

I have fought a good fight, I have finished my course, I have kept the faith: Henceforth there is laid up for me a crown of righteousness, which the Lord, the righteous judge, shall give me at that day: and not to me only, but unto all them also that love his appearing.

[2 Timothy 4:7-8 AV]

It is a source of great sadness to me that some people feel it arrogant to *know* you will go to heaven, to *know* you are forgiven. It is a very English heresy that insists that, in part at least, we must earn our salvation; that has the effrontery to suggest that Jesus' death on the cross was somehow deficient.

The Christian faith, my mother's faith, is expressed very clearly by Paul when writing to the Ephesians in these words:

For by grace are ye saved through faith; and that not of yourselves: it is the gift of God: Not of works, lest any man should boast. For we are his workmanship, created in Christ Jesus unto good works, which God hath before ordained that we should walk in them.

[Ephesians 2:8-10 AV]

The week we announced our engagement her parents announced their intention to separate. I don't think the two events were linked! Many people here in this church have felt too the pain and distress of a marriage that has ended, or has become broken beyond repair. So, what does the Bible say?

Firstly, in the Old Testament, it is clear right at the beginning that God created us for relationships – with him and with each other. We are made physically, psychologically and emotionally to give and receive love. As Dr Patrick Dixon, a south London church leader, a medical doctor and director of a church-based charity, Aids Care Education and Training, said in a recent seminar on teenage sexuality: 'We are made for friendship, fellowship and in some cases, fusion.' In Genesis 2:24, there are the three stages of 'leaving, cleaving and one flesh' involved in the traditional model of marriage. However, by the time of Moses, it was clear that not all marriages were surviving – some were broken and others were breaking. Why? Because we live in a fallen world and are selfish people at heart.

Broken relationships are one of the chief consequences of sin. Our relationship with God is broken but so also are our relationships with each other. Hence Deuteronomy 24:1-4. From this we see four things. Firstly, divorce is God's concession to the world in which we live but it is not his ideal. Secondly, there was a need for some civil legislation in order to bring some sort of order to society. Thirdly, there needed to be some provision in order to protect the women concerned and fourthly, remarriage was allowed. It was no light or easy matter however. The Hebrew word for 'divorce' is the same word used for the cutting down of a tree. It envisages the severing of a living union. It is a kind of amputation that cannot occur without damage to the partners concerned. If you know anything about divorce, you'll know how true that is.

Divorce then is not encouraged in the Old Testament but is recognized. However, we need to remember Malachi 2:14-16 where God says clearly that he hates divorce. But please do note what God *doesn't* say. He *doesn't* say that he hates the divorcee. Sadly so many comments and asides can give the impression that Christians hate *people* who get divorced. That is not the case. They need love, understanding, and acceptance rather than condemnation.

It is sobering to think that it is the same God who speaks through Malachi who also tells Hosea to marry a prostitute, as an illustration of his relationship with the people of Israel and who, following repentance, promises through Jeremiah to heal and forgive the Israelites for divorcing him.

It was into this debate about divorce that Jesus came. At the time of his ministry, there were two rabbis giving very different advice. One, named Rabbi Shammai, advised that divorce was only allowable following serious sexual sin. Rabbi Hillel, on the other hand, was of the opinion that divorce could be granted for any reason – a wife's bad cooking, a funny look at her husband, or just on the whim of the husband. Men's attitudes to women at this time were often aggressive and callous – on the open market a good cow would often bring a higher price than a woman!

So it was that Jesus was tested by the Pharisees. In Matthew 19, he refuses to enter into the debate between the two rabbis but rather reinforces the traditional teaching on marriage. He affirms that marriage was: designed by God (v. 4); complementary (v. 4); permanent (v. 5); exclusive (v. 5); nuclear (v. 5); and not for everyone (vv.10-12). It is good to reflect that we have no inherent right to get married *once*, never mind *twice*.

Jesus dissociates himself from both Hillel *and* Shammai. He declares Moses' provision of divorce to be a temporary concession to human sin – stating 'your hearts were hard'. He argues against legalism. It is clear Jesus is against divorce and remarriage *but...but* we live in a fallen world. The Jesus of John 8:1-11, a passage we'll look at later in our series, shows a Jesus of forgiveness and compassion.

> Has no one condemned you?...Then neither do I condemn
> you. Go now and leave your life of sin.

Please hear what Jesus is saying and what I have said. Divorce is *not* God's ideal. He hates it and his plan is for marriage to be a lifelong commitment. But in the Old Testament, divorce and remarriage are allowed and in the New Testament, in 1 Corinthians, Paul permits remarriage if a Christian's partner dies and they remarry a Christian.

Please note that it is God's plan for Christians to marry Christians. You cannot marry someone who is not a Christian without one of your two relationships, either with God or your partner, suffering as a result. (If you are married to someone who isn't a Christian, Paul advises you stay with them and love them into the Kingdom of God.)

Divorce then is a concession to our fallen world. Like all the consequences of sin, it brings pain and guilt, suffering and misunderstanding, sadness and loneliness. But it is not the end. If attempts at reconciliation fail – and they need to be pursued with Relate or some other counsellor – and divorce does happen, it is *not* the unforgivable sin. There is a chance of a new start and a new beginning. That is what the Gospel is all about. There will need to be repentance which may well have to be made public. One of the healthiest wedding services I have ever attended was one in which one of the partners was a divorcee. Having become a Christian since his marriage failed, he was challenged at the start of the service by the officiating minister to acknowledge his share of the blame involved for the failure of his first marriage. He was asked if he repented of his part in the break up of his first marriage, which he did, and the rest of the marriage then proceeded. It had obviously followed many hours of discussion and prayer but made sense of the service about to begin.

We all need to repent and acknowledge our failure to live up to God's standards and expectations. We would do well to remember that there is no league table of sin. Sexual sin seems to be regarded as worse than any other and though its consequences may be more damaging and long lasting, God views *all* sin as equally bad. We all need to repent and when it comes to divorce and remarriage, dare we cast the first stone?

Love and Sexuality

Sermon preached by John Irvine at St Barnabas Church, Kensington, London, on 23 October 1994.

Mr Irvine, ordained in 1981 after six years as a barrister specializing in crime, has been Vicar of St Barnabas since last year. From 1985 he was priest-in-charge of the church, which had a small congregation of fifteen but grew overnight to more than 100 when he moved with a group from Holy Trinity, Brompton, in Knightsbridge in the first of that church's successful 'plants'. Mr Irvine, married with four children, has since seen the congregation grow to nearly 600 over three Sunday services. He says: 'Preaching is very important as communicating God's truth through the expounding of his word to the changing of people's lives. We believe that the Bible is God's authoritative word for today. It is already relevant to today, but it is the preacher's job to bring out its meaning and to apply it to today's situations.'

Bible text: Matthew 19:1-12

Tonight we are looking at another interesting subject, Jesus and sex, and we are looking at these subjects as one particular Gospel deals with them, the Gospel of Matthew. Of course, few people would say that Jesus had much to say about sex. I was hearing only this morning someone whose flatmate said to them: 'Well, what on earth is he going to say?' And fewer still would think that vicars have much to say about the subject of sex. There are those who think that there are three sexes in the world: men, women and vicars.

One vicar was recently asked to come and talk to a local girls' school about sex and he was very embarrassed but said yes. He was so embarrassed that when his wife asked him what he was going to speak about, rather than acknowledge the true subject, he said the first thing that came into his mind: 'sailing'. She thought that was a bit odd, but didn't say anything, saw him afterwards, asked how it went and he said it was fine thank you. The following day she ran into the headmistress in Sainsbury's and the headmistress was kind enough and polite enough to say, 'Your husband gave the most wonderful talk.' 'Did he really!' she replied. 'He doesn't know much about it, you know. He's only done it twice. The first time he was as sick as a dog and the second time his hat blew off.' That's one of those risky stories that I love but can only tell when I'm speaking on this subject.

The fact is that Jesus was not embarrassed by sex. He happily talked to the immoral woman at the well, he enjoyed the company of prostitutes and obviously felt at ease with them, and he refused to condemn the woman caught in adultery. Here we see that he's involved in the healing ministry. He's moved from Galilee, ministering in the power of the Spirit, and then some big shots come up with a loaded question (verse 3). Ostensibly it's about divorce, but the reality is that it's a trap. In effect it's saying 'which side are you on in this hot potato of an issue that is everyone's talking point at the moment?' And Jesus refuses to be bound by the negative agenda that these people are wanting to set him. And instead he says some important things, some positive things as well as some negative things. And I want to underline four of those tonight, from verse 4 and following.

And the first is this wonderful truth that we need to hear again and again, and that is that *sex is good*. Look at verse 4. Jesus replied. 'Stop coming in on questions of divorce. Haven't you read that at the beginning the Creator made them male and female?' In other words, sex was God's idea. Sex was God's idea from the beginning. Sex did not come in as a result of the Fall. It was not a consequence of sin. It was God Almighty's plan right at the start to create a world that involved sexuality. Jesus points back to the beginning and says a perfect God decides on creating a good world and sexuality and sex was part of that goodness, part of that world. And the reason we need to keep underlining that truth and keep reminding ourselves of it, is that the sad fact is that the Church has often not given that impression. It prefers not to mention the subject by and large, and when it does the picture that it gives is of an embarrassing, rather sordid thing that's necessary for procreation, but otherwise let's try and avoid it. And Jesus is saying that's a travesty. He points them back to the beginning and he quotes from Genesis. And you'll remember the story. Adam had named all the animals but he's feeling nonetheless just a bit disappointed and lonely. And God's response is: 'It's not good for the man to remain alone. I will make a helper suitable for him.' And so he makes woman. And at the first wedding in history, Genesis describes how God brought her to Adam. He gives her away. And Adam's response was: 'Wow! This is what I've been waiting for, this is good.' And as lovers ever since have done, he breaks into poetry: 'Bone of my bone, flesh of my flesh, she shall be called woman for she was taken out of me.' Not very good poetry, but that doesn't matter. They were brought together and they were united. And this passage that Jesus refers to says that they felt no shame in their nakedness. That's how good sex is, that's how good sex is meant to be.

But secondly, we see that *sex is for marriage*. Look at verse 5. Quoting Genesis again, Jesus says, 'For this reason a man will leave his father and mother and be united to his wife and the two will become one flesh so they are no longer two but one.' It's amazing truth. It's extraordinary, but the Bible teaches it clearly from the beginning that when two people get married, in a very real sense, in the spiritual realms, in the heavenly places, as far as God is concerned, at that moment they become one. They may not feel like it immediately, but in God's sight they are one and their marriage is a living out of what is true in the heavenly places. It's just like becoming a Christian. When people first come to Christ, often they don't necessarily feel very different. But the moment they make a commitment to Jesus, they pass from darkness to light, from death to life. That is true in the heavenly realms, and then they have to live it out in practice. And gradually what happens is what is true in heaven becomes true in our experience. Likewise as far as marriage is concerned. And that's why God hates divorce. It is because divorce is tearing apart that which God has joined together and made one. Sexual intercourse is both the symbol and the practical reality of that oneness. Sex is very bonding. That's how God designed it. It is the glue in marriage. To have sex with anyone is to bond and that's why it only makes sense to bond with one you are committed to for life. That kind of bonding only makes sense within the context and the security and the commitment of faithful, monogamous marriage. Now, it's not surprising that because God designed it that way, the best sex is enjoyed within marriage. All the stuff that the world presents, that the best sex is outside marriage, is actually a lie. I thought I'd bring along some of my reading material tonight. One periodical that I enjoy is *The Economist* and last week I opened it up and my eye caught for some reason page 62, an American survey: 'New Sex Study Shock'. Goodness, I thought, will this be relevant? Hurriedly I turned to page 62, wondering whether I should go out and destroy all copies of *The Economist*. But do you know what they are talking about? You've probably read about this in the press elsewhere: they're absolutely amazed, there's been a new survey, you see, and this isn't just interviewing boastful volunteers, this is a genuine random sample. And the amazing thing is that they are finding that night after night all over America, faithfully monogamous couples, of different gender, enjoy sex together. Sex shock indeed. The thing they really can't understand – honestly I'm not making this up – is why Protestant fundamentalist women have orgasms with exceptional frequency. Research is showing that Christians enjoy sex because *that's* how it's meant to be enjoyed, within the security and commitment of faith and relationship with God and commitment to one another. That makes for good sex. So if you are married tonight, I want to encourage you with all my heart to invest in that side of your relationship. It's not just an addition, it's not just an extra. It's vital to your relationship. It's the glue, keep investing in it. And it's so easy for it to get squeezed out, from exhaustion or work, so that we don't allow time and energy to that very important ingredient.

Sex is good. Sex for marriage. Thirdly, *illicit sex is destructive*. Verse 6: 'Therefore what God has joined together, let man not separate.' It couldn't be clearer. We cannot get round this. Jesus is stating absolutely that adultery is out. Why? Because it is tearing apart what Almighty God has joined together and it's destructive. And I'm so sorry that my other reading material has such an obvious example. According to the *Sunday Times* today, the heir to the throne acknowledges in his authorized biography an intimate sexual affair outside his marriage. Now I'm not throwing stones and it must be a terrible thing to be locked into a loveless marriage and I don't want to be condemning at all, and yet it's a frightening example of how destructive illicit sex can be anywhere. And it's no good trying to make it acceptable by having legal papers of divorce, except for persistent unfaithfulness, says Jesus, and then remarrying in an attempt to legalize sex, that is still adultery, says Jesus, verse 9. It's tough isn't it? But that's what Jesus says. And I'm in the business of telling you what Jesus says.

Elsewhere, Jesus specifically condemns sexual immorality. In this Gospel for example, chapter 15:19, that would include fornication, that's sexual intercourse before marriage, and homosexual practice. Jesus doesn't forbid sex in the circumstances I'm describing just to be a killjoy or to rob us of fun. He was a fun-loving party-goer. He forbids this to protect us from the destruction that goes with it. I was trying to think of an illustration, and for some reasons found myself thinking of a racing car. Now a racing car is a powerful thing and a wonderful thing, I'm sure, to watch, if you're interested in that sort of thing, in the right context. In other words, on a race track it is a joy to behold and experience. But to let my daughter loose in it, for example, would not only be dangerous, it would be destructive, because it's not designed for her to use, and she's not designed for it. Do you see what I'm saying? It's not a negative comment on her and it's certainly not a negative comment about racing cars. It is just a sensible truth. Now sex is more powerful than any racing car. But outside the marriage bed, it's as destructive as a racing car let loose in the wrong hands. Although that's clear, there are some grey areas. Adultery, actual homosexual practice, fornication, bestiality – these things are clearly destructive, but there are some things which aren't so clear: heavy petting is one. Is heavy petting illicit sex? And the answer is, not if you're married. If you're involved with a Christian friend and into heavy petting, then you need to be careful because heavy petting is designed to lead to intercourse itself and so you're on dangerous ground trying to call a halt. If you're involved in that level of intimacy with a Christian friend, I advise you take a step back, to sit down and talk together and agree your guidelines as to what could be helpful for your relationship so that you don't bond too quickly and rush into decisions that might be unwise. If you're involved in heavy petting with a non-Christian, then end the relationship immediately!

One question also that often arises is: 'Is masturbation illicit sex?' And the answer is that neither Jesus nor the Bible specifically mention it, and therefore the one thing that we can be sure of is that it's not the highest of God's priorities. Having said that, it's not exactly loving and giving as sex in marriage is meant to be. It tends to be linked with fantasy. It's what Martin Luther called, and I think it's a good phrase, a 'puppy sin'. It's a sin of immaturity – not to be encouraged or ignored, but neither is it to be something to get in a great stew over. That's the work of the enemy. So don't beat yourself up over it, just grow up, put it behind you and get on with the stuff of life.

I think it's good to remember with all illicit sex, that like any sin, it can be forgiven. Whatever your past failure, or your present wrong behaviour, God can forgive you and God longs to forgive you. There's nothing more he wants to do tonight if you're in that situation. The likelihood, quite honestly, must be, mustn't it, in a gathering of this size, with so many young people present, that there will be a good many of us who have, in the past, failed in our own standards, let alone God's standards, who are aware of having hurt ourselves and who are perhaps feeling guilty or feeling bad about it, or who are presently involved in something we know is not right. Well, don't go away feeling still burdened by that. Take advantage this evening of putting things right with God, because that is what he longs for you to do. He longs for you to bring it to him that it might be dealt with, that you might be washed as clean as the whitest snow and go on from here in purity and right relationship with him. He gives you his Holy Spirit which not only makes you his temple but gives you the power to follow his way.

There's one more thing that Jesus stresses. And that is that if illicit sex is destructive, *singleness can be constructive*. Look at verse 10. The disciples try and joke about Jesus' hard teaching. Perhaps it's better not to marry, ho ho! Jesus takes that point seriously. They were hoping that he would say, 'Oh, no, no, no, no, I'm not saying that.' But what Jesus says in verse 11 is:

> Not everyone can accept this word but only those to whom
> it's been given. Some are eunuchs because they are born
> that way, others because they are made that way by men,
> and others have renounced marriage because of the
> kingdom of heaven. The one who can accept this should
> accept it.

Marriage is a wonderful thing but it is not the be all and end all. Sex is great but it's not the greatest. It can't be. There won't be any sex in heaven. You don't have to experience sex to be fulfilled. Jesus was a full-blooded man. The most complete, the most wonderful man there has ever been and yet the fact is that our trail-blazer, the first human into heaven, was a virgin, and the truth is that sex and marriage make demands on time, energy and priorities that can and do compete with the Kingdom. Correspondingly, a single person in time and energy and lack of other commitments can serve and give himself and herself to the Kingdom more fully. In other words, all that Jesus is saying here is blessing those who, like him, are willing to sacrifice sexual fulfilment in order to serve the Kingdom. I wonder whether there are any here in that category tonight? Of course, the world and the Church combined can often make it difficult to follow that calling. The world and the Church often make it seem that marriage is the only way. I know one dear person who is a wonderful Christian, but every time I talk to her she is always praying for this or that person because they will never be fulfilled until they are married; and it seems to me that's a wrong way of looking at it. But I know one or two, they are few in number: I can think of two obvious examples, great people in my estimation, who have consciously, before God, sacrificed marriage in order to give themselves to the Kingdom. God in his goodness didn't call me that way. He knew that I probably couldn't cope. But again, it's likely, isn't it, that there will be one or two here in that category and all I'm wanting to say is what Jesus would say to you, if you're in that category: God bless you. Don't feel that you are a complete crazy weirdo. Sex is good, but the Kingdom is best. Sex is temporary. The Kingdom is eternal.

Let's be quiet and pray.

Available to the Controller

Sermon preached by Alex Gunn at Aberfeldy parish church, Perthshire, on 7 August 1994.

Mr Gunn, 52, married with two children, is also minister at Amulree, Strathbraan, Dull and Weem Parish Churches. He was ordained at 24 after an MA and BD at Edinburgh. He was Convener of the Church of Scotland working party that produced a report on rural areas in Scotland, and argued the case for a worshipping fellowship in each natural community, no matter how small. In his own church at Amulree, the average attendance is nine. 'It is important in preaching not to try to make the Christian faith relevant or up to date, but to show that it already is, in that it is objectively true in history and meets the basic needs of people today.'

Bible text: Romans 12:1-2

London's Burning, a television series, has a high rating. Through it folk enter into the traumas faced by firemen. Have you been involved in a fire?

I remember going into a bad fire and envying the firemen when they came. I was coughing and spluttering, scarcely able to get a breath because of the poisonous fumes, losing all sense of direction in the blinding smoke. But when the firemen came, they could cope. They were not dependent on the atmosphere round about, but on an inner air supply, through their breathing apparatus sets. And through their guideline they were connected up to safety.

A Christian is like the fireman. Being a Christian is not escapism from the problems of life – indeed a Christian is called to go in to deal with problems. But a Christian is not dependent on circumstances or the attitudes in society which poison thinking and relationships – for a

Christian breathes by means of a special spiritual air supply, and knows that ultimately he is connected to safety in Christ.

That is the picture we have of Christians at the beginning of Romans, chapter 12: of Christians *not conforming* (and the word is used of being moulded like a jelly!) *to the world*, that is, society being run without reference to God, but *being transformed by the renewal of our minds.*

Renewal. We hear of the renewal of derelict inner cities: the Christian faith is about renewal of men and women who may be hurting, helpless, with no sense of direction. How?

There are two words for 'new' in the Greek: one is new, meaning latest, and the other is new, meaning fresh, clean, having a distinctive quality, not dependent on circumstances. It is usually this second one which is used to describe Christians, the 'new creatures' Christ makes us, as Paul tells the church in Corinth.

Now Corinth had a bad reputation – we speak of 'going to the dogs'; in the first century they spoke of 'going to Corinth'. Paul wrote to the early Christians in Corinth, that most permissive of cities, at a time when many of them were experiencing problems of illness and death. He speaks of the distinctive difference the new quality of life makes to what otherwise is mere existence:

> We are under pressure, but not cornered; at our wit's end, but not our hope's end; pushed down by man, but never let down by God; knocked down, but not knocked out...so we do not lose heart. Though our outer nature be wasting away, our inner nature is renewed day by day...while we look, not to the things that are seen, but to the things that are not seen. The things that are seen are passing, the things that are not seen are eternal – and are made known in Jesus Christ !
>
> [2 Corinthians 4:8-9, 16, 18]

This renewing means that while Christians may feel pressures, we are lifted above dependence on what is happening either in society or in physical health: being renewed means that we are not just reactors, mere victims of circumstances – we matter to God. Paul experienced God at work in him, even when he was in prison because of his faith.

It is this fresh distinctive quality which God wants us to have.

Do we want to have what God wants to give us?
Renewal is possible because of *the Resource.*

This letter to the church in the capital of the Roman Empire is laid out logically, as can be seen by the four sections, each of which starts with the word 'Therefore':

Romans 2:1   Therefore all have sinned...
Romans 5:1   Therefore it is by what God has done, received by faith that our contact with God is restored...
Romans 8:1   Therefore Christians depend on God's Spirit...
Romans 12:1 Therefore, in view of the mercy of God...that is, in view of all that is described in the previous chapters.

Christian commitment is a logical response to the truth of God revealed in Jesus Christ whereby we enter into a relationship of commitment to the living God and of the alignment of our lives to his will as we are empowered by his Spirit working in and through us.

When a fireman starts each new watch, one of his first actions is to check the tally on the breathing apparatus set to ensure that it is filled: so too Christians will want to ensure that our minds are constantly being filled both with the information of the good news of Jesus Christ and with the power of the Holy Spirit who makes that information come alive, so renewing our minds.

He is our resource. How is our tally showing?
But is not this talk of God renewing and resourcing us a bit selfish? Far from it – look at *the Result.*

In the rest of the chapter there are detailed examples of the working out of what God is working in the life of the Christian. The rest of Romans chapter 12 goes on to give practical examples of the life-style generated by the new life:

having gifts that differ let us use them
    serving, teaching, encouraging, contributing, helping
let love be genuine

> rejoice in your hope
> be patient in trouble
> practise hospitality
> rejoice with those who rejoice, weep with those who weep
> live in harmony with one another.

New life leads to a new life-style. These examples are based on the principles contained in verses one and two, which indicate that the ultimate logic of the Gospel message is that Christians are available for the *will of God*.

When Bravo 261, our local fire appliance, returns after an incident, the crew reports to their controller that they are 'at Bravo 6 and *available*'. Firemen work as individuals and as a team in contact with and available for use by their controller.

Available to the controller: verse 11 speaks of 'serving the Lord'. The key to it all is our understanding of the nature of 'the Lord', for

> although He's the Lord of all glory,
> yet He's only a prayer away.

But all too often the word 'Lord' conjures up a somewhat dated irrelevant dignitary, who meets with others in a group which some people would like to see abolished! The picture in the letter to the church at Rome – and the whole Bible for that matter – sees the 'Lord' as a dynamic controller: Creator of the universe, who has defeated death and evil, as evidenced by the cross and resurrection; and so is able to re-create the world by re-creating people through *renewing* and *resourcing, resulting in people available for his service*, as the 'love of Christ controls us', as was found in Corinth (2 Corinthians 5:14).

Are we available for God, the ultimate controller?
Nothing could be more thrilling!

> Therefore in view of God's mercy, offer yourselves as a living sacrifice, holy and acceptable to God which is your reasonable service. Do not be conformed to this world, but be transformed by the renewal of your mind, that you may prove what is the will of God.
>
> [Romans 12]

God Among Us

Sermon preached by John Thomson at St Mary's, Wheatley, Doncaster, on 2 October 1994.

John, who trained at Wycliffe Hall, Oxford, and in South Africa was ordained deacon in 1985 and priested the following year. Previously he gained a degree at York University, worked as an auxiliary nurse and as a parish assistant, and has done factory and labourers' jobs. John, married with two children and completing his first book, Why Bother with Church? *says: 'Preaching connects the world of the Bible with the world of today. What I try to do when preaching is to imagine the context of my hearers, investigate the passage or theme in terms of its own context, and seek through the sermon to bring the two together using images, pictures and stories to give colour.'*

Bible text: Acts 2:37-47

> Customers of the McDonald's opposite Liverpool Street Station in London will doubtless be suprised to learn that the big, amiable American with swept back fair hair who approached them recently to ask if they enjoyed their meal was not a restaurant employee but Michael Quinlan, chairman and chief executive of the McDonald's Corporation.
>
> [*The Times*, 30 September 1994]

It's twenty years since the Gospel or 'Good News' of McDonald's hit the UK. Twenty years of hamburgers, french fries, milkshakes, the lot (and they're quite tasty, I must admit), but isn't it remarkable that at the centre of this McDonald's gospel train is a leader willing to walk anonymously among his customers and engage with them without the trappings of status and of power!

Today our theme is 'The Gospel – Old and New'. For Peter and the earliest Christians, the Gospel was about recognizing God hidden among us in the figure of Jesus the carpenter preacher and having our lives transformed by our *repentance* or *change of mind* about him.

This was the experience of that crowd of folk who heard Peter preach the first Christian sermon. They knew of Jesus, the preacher from Galilee who had recently been executed for subversion, but as Peter shared with them the reason why the disciples were so radiant and worshipping God in all sorts of foreign languages they began to *see Jesus in a different light*. What they had thought and believed before was *inadequate*. This *Jesus was no nobody but instead the Messiah, God's Saviour amongst them*. In Peter's words:

> Let all the house of Israel therefore know that God has
> made Him both Lord and Christ.
>
> [Acts 2:36]

I enjoy looking at optical illusions. One I most like appears on first sight to be an ordinary rustic scene, with clouds, a forest, hills and a pond. However upon closer inspection one can see the face of a woman shaped by the contours of the hills against the sky. Looking at the picture in a new light reveals its deeper secret.

The Gospel is first and foremost about discovering the secret of *who Jesus is*. It is realizing that he is no simple romantic teacher of religious truths but is rather *God among us*. It is about realizing that God is indeed *here*...that God can be known in our terms, that God is available to all.

Such a realization cannot but cut us to the quick. We can no longer live as we did before. *If Jesus is indeed God among us then our life can no longer be lived as if that didn't matter.*

Seeing Jesus in a new light immediately sheds light upon our lives. Like the crowd we find ourselves asking: *'What then must we do?'*

I love Tom and Jerry cartoons. Often you'll find that Tom dresses up or hides in such a way that Jerry wanders around unaware of his presence when suddenly Tom appears and Jerry recognizes him. When this happens, Jerry doesn't just carry on as if nothing has happened! He changes into top gear and screeches out of sight.

We cannot stay the same if we really believe that Jesus is God among us. Our lives have to change. As Peter says:

'Repent and be baptized, every one of you, in the name of
Jesus Christ for the forgiveness of your sins; and you shall
recieve the gift of the Holy Spirit...'

[Acts 2:38 RSV]

What Peter is saying is that now our whole life has to be offered back
to Jesus.

First, we rethink our lives by saying: 'If Jesus is God among us,
then I must worship him with all that I am...I cannot do any
less...Jesus becomes my first concern and commitment in life...I live
my life for him...I am now his servant.' This is repentance.

Second, we get baptized. We go through a public ceremony of
commitment that says to everyone around us: 'I now belong to Jesus. I
carry his mark, the cross, on me day by day and I will live my life as
someone who belongs to Jesus whatever happens.' This is
discipleship.

Third, we receive forgiveness and the Holy Spirit. God embraces us
as his children and gives us his own Spirit, his living presence in our
lives to assure us that we are his and to empower us to follow Jesus
faithfully. This is empowerment.

The Gospel, or seeing Jesus in a new light, transforms how we live
and act. Henceforth we are set free to live for God. Life no longer is
simply a private struggle within an ambiguous world. It is a shared
journey with the Creator of the world.

The resources we need to contend with life's traumas as well as
life's joys are no longer unilaterally mustered. Instead we find
suprising energies become available to us from beyond ourselves.

The evidence of the truth of this Gospel becomes apparent in the
reorientation of our lives. We are joined by a pilot who continually
hints at the most appropriate channels to sail in.

When we see Jesus as God and when we commit ourselves to him
we find ourselves in a new family. What is interesting is that those
early Christians didn't simply content themselves with belonging, for
in verse 42 we read:

They devoted themselves to the apostles' teaching and
fellowship, to the breaking of bread and the prayers.

For the person who has seen Jesus and themselves in the light of
the Gospel, church ceases to be an optional extra and is instead

absolutely essential if we are to grow up as Christians.

Since my children were born they have grown up watching and copying us. They have spent time with us. They have eaten with us. They have spoken to us. To date their lives have been crucially shaped by us.

As we see Jesus as Lord and reorientate our lives to his service, we discover the value of the experience, support, fellowship and strength of his family. Warts and all, it becomes for us a critical community.

In a recent interview with the *Church Times*, the Labour Party leader, Tony Blair, himself a practising Anglican, said this: 'In reality the Christian message is that the self is best realised through communion with others. The act of Holy Communion is symbolic of this message. It acknowledges that we do not grow up in total independence, but interdependently' [30 September 1994].

The Gospel is about realizing that we must belong and be devoted to discovering God's will for our lives in and through our church.

It is twenty years since the Gospel of the Big Mac came to Britain. It's almost two thousand years since the Gospel of Jesus Christ came to life in Palestine.

That Gospel has transformed millions of people's lives and it will do so for us if we too discover this:

New way of seeing Jesus...he is the Lord.

New way of seeing ourselves...we are his servants.

New way of seeing the Church... we are his people.

Risen Lord Jesus, you are our Lord. We offer our lives to you and our church to you this day and forever, Amen.

Time

Sermon preached by Stephen Knowers at St Peter's, Croydon, on 27 November 1994.

Stephen, 45, married with two children, moved to St Peter's last year after working as Chaplain at Southbank University. He was ordained in 1973 after taking a degree in Theology at King's College, London. Stephen has a special interest in the politics and culture of Estonia because his wife, Kersti, comes from Estonia. They met in a disco when he was on holiday by the Black Sea. After months of negotiations and a marriage in Estonia, she was able to come to this country and now works as a film-maker. Stephen says 'Preaching is the bread and butter of priests and ministers up and down the country. It is the main way in which we communicate with people. We should probably give preaching more consideration because, whatever other ways we use to communicate with people, most people hear us when we preach.'

Do you remember the first time you went to the sea and saw the horizon? I was with my Dad. We were having a picnic above the cliffs at Folkestone. When he told me that what I could see quite plainly was not, in fact, the edge of the world, I didn't believe him. He explained that the world was not a plate, but a ball. But it wasn't until I was older, when I saw pictures taken from space, that I realized that my Dad was telling the truth.

That first lesson prepared me for a later time when I heard that the Milky Way wasn't the misty line of stars it seemed to be, but a great spiralling wheel of stars, of which our sun was one. It looked flat because we were a part of it.

Still later I heard that the universe itself was round and that if I could travel for an unimaginably long time, I would eventually come back, like the great navigators, to where I'd started from.

And as if that wasn't enough, it seems that time is also like a wheel. There's nothing new about this idea. In fact it's probably the oldest way of telling the time. After all, doesn't the rising and setting sun look as if it's going round the world? Doesn't the moon wax and wane once a month? Don't the seasons turn full circle every year? And the crops we live on too? Perhaps that's why the prehistoric people of Britain built Stonehenge in the shape of a wheel. Perhaps that's why our clocks (at least the old-fashioned ones) are shaped like wheels too.

This idea that time is like a wheel is beautifully expressed in the book of Ecclesiastes, chapter 3:

> For everything its season,
> and for every activity under heaven its time:
>
> a time to be born and a time to die;
> a time to plant and a time to uproot;
> a time to kill and a time to heal;
> a time to pull down and a time to build up;
> a time to weep and a time to laugh;
> a time for mourning and a time for dancing;
> a time to scatter stones and a time to gather them;
> a time to embrace and a time to refrain from embracing;
> a time to seek and a time to lose;
> a time to keep and a time to throw away;
> a time to tear and a time to mend;
> a time for silence and a time for speech...
>
> [Ecclesiastes 3:1-7 NEB]

The person who wrote Ecclesiastes is immersed in his idea of time as a great wheel. He seems to our ears to be rather complacent, cynical even. And Westerners literally don't have much time for the more slow moving fatalistic civilizations of the world. But there's also something calming about those words. They seem to say: 'Don't panic, there's time for everything and if there's not time now, there will be if you're patient enough to wait.'

In the New Testament there's a special Greek word for this kind of time – *chronos*, from which our word 'chronicle' comes. This is the sort of time wise men can read from the night sky. King Herod asks the wise men what *chronos* time the Bethlehem star appeared. This is the sort of time that describes the predictable period of carrying an unborn child. The *chronos* time comes for Elizabeth's child, John the Baptist, to be born.

There's a wheel on the flag of the Republic of India. On the face of it, it seems to represent *chronos* time, and the many births of the Hindu way and the patience of the people of India. But the wheel on the Indian flag isn't there for that reason; its there to commemorate a moment in the history of India when her people were impatient for change and for freedom: a moment when in response to the prompting of Mahatma Gandhi, they took to their spinning-wheels to destroy the dependency of India on the cotton-mills of Lancashire. The wheel isn't always what it seems to be. On the flag of India, its spinning-wheel is a sign, not of fatalism, but of peaceful revolution.

The New Testament has another word for this kind of time – *kairos* time. It means 'moment of truth'. There are moments of time that won't come again; there are opportunities not to be missed, invitations to a great banquet to be replied to, oil to be put aside just in case. There's an urgency about the Gospel call to us. 'Now,' wrote the apostle, 'now is the time [the *kairos* time] to awake out of sleep.'

Christians believe that God, who is eternal, chose to show his love for us in time. He made a universe for us out of nothing, and made time too. The universe is old by our standards and may well grow older, but in the end there will be an end, and it will be God's, as the beginning was God's too.

But that isn't all. Christians also believe that our eternal God has stepped into this universe, here on this planet in Jesus Christ. This was his *kairos* moment, a rare moment, a unique moment.

In Christ, God has come to us in one particular person, in one particular place, at one particular time and he speaks to us from that moment with the urgency of one who loves in a vulnerable way. In Jesus, God has put himself into our hands. In Jesus, God took the risk that we might miss that moment and pass by on the other side. In Jesus, God went to his cross, just once and only once, and part of his pain outside that city wall was that his loved-ones might not see that in this ugly death was a blood-stained invitation to life.

But God didn't begin to love us from the cross. He loved us from the first star-dust moment of creation, from the dividing of the first cell. He knew each of us in our mother's womb. But we didn't know. We didn't know he loved us. We breathed, but we didn't know why. We didn't even know that there could be a reason.

When a great tree is cut down in the forest, and you look at its severed trunk, you can read the story of the tree. When the tree stood erect, its story seemed to be in its height, its strength and its beauty. But when it is cut down, you can read its story in the rings within its trunk: for each year, another ring. At least, they look like rings to us, but, in fact, they reach from the base of the trunk to its top. The tree tells the story of the changing seasons in its trunk. To the experienced eye it tells even of the climatic changes during its lifetime.

This is just what we see in the life of Jesus. This giving, this teaching, this suffering, that we see in the lifetime of Jesus is severing the trunk of time, slicing the wheel of inevitability in two. In Jesus, we see what was always God's way with his creation. The giving that brought redemption in Jesus was always there, but we ignored the prophets and never knew. Even before the first human beings walked the earth, our Creator was loving through the rocks and the plants and the ocean. They were his prophets then, and still God takes moments of time and speaks through words and acts that we can understand, of eternal things, things which our minds will never grasp.

Every time a man or a woman is baptized, the trunk of eternity is severed again, and we see in a moment of time, the eternal love and justice of God. Your maker didn't start to love you when you or those you love said 'Yes' to him in the promises of baptism. He always loved you. He always knew you. But there had to come a moment of truth, when you saw that you belonged and the creature spoke and said 'Yes'. And you, who were always his son or daughter, became 'adopted' as the child of God you always were. In baptism the trunk of God's providence is cut in two and we see that what was always true, is true for us too.

But there was one moment in time that wasn't inevitable, one mighty act of God that didn't have to happen. For all the cut flowers of Easter, the rabbits, the eggs, the signs of new life that seem to say that this Resurrection was as predictable as the next spring, it didn't have to be. When God raised Jesus from the dead, he did so in a moment of *kairos* time. The spring is as old as the spinning planet, but the Resurrection is a divine surprise. We, inheritors of Resurrection, are invited by Christ into this movement of divine surprise. For us too, there will be moments of *kairos* time, and our life in Christ is a preparation for those moments.

In 1985, 150 ministers of all races in South Africa issued the Kairos Declaration. They called their fellow Christians out of complacency to recognize the moment to which God had brought them. The God of the Bible, they said, wasn't the God 'who exalts the proud and humbles the poor'. He was the God who 'scatters the proud of heart, pulls down the mighty from their thrones and exalts the humble'.

There is a time to plant and a time to uproot. May our God who made time, make us tellers of the time, that each of us may know when to tear and when to mend; when to remain silent and when to speak.

Understanding the Times

Sermon preached by Sean Carter at Clipston Baptist Church, Northamptonshire, on 15 January 1995.

Sean Carter, 26, has been in full-time ministry for 18 months. He entered the Royal Navy at 16 in 1985, and from the age of 20 was working on the cross-channel ferries as an engineer. He was brought up a Pentecostal, drifted away as a teenager and when he was 20 he had a conversion experience after people began to share their faith with him. He was preaching for five years before his induction as the pastor of his church. His church produces videos and audio-tapes, and has a congregation of both elderly and young. He says 'Preaching is a very good way of communicating the Gospel of Jesus Christ. The spoken word is as effective as it always has been, and preaching has an important part in teaching about morals and values as well as proclaiming the Christian Gospel.'

Bible text: 1 Chronicles 12:32

> Men of Issachar...understood the times and knew what Israel should do, two hundred chiefs with all their relatives under their command.

Let's pray for the Lord's blessing upon his word.

> Heavenly Father, as we look at the message which you have given to me this morning to share with the believers here Lord, we pray for your power and presence to be amongst us and we pray, Lord God, that we will understand the times which we are living in as the Church and we just pray, Lord God, that you will bless each and every person here this morning; in Jesus's name we pray. Amen.

This one verse in the Old Testament was during a time of great turmoil and a time of great national strife and war when Saul had just been killed on Mount Gilboa by the Philistines. They had this great battle and Saul had to commit suicide because his army was devastated, his army was destroyed and the Bible tells us that Saul killed himself by falling upon his sword. And these men who had followed Saul and followed the Philistines, they started to understand that a change had come, that a new season had come upon their nation, that David was the man who was to be the next King, that David was the man who God had chosen to be King. And they started all flocking over to David.

When you get home, if you read the rest of that twelfth chapter you will see that all of the people were coming to David in their thousands. The tribes of Israel were suddenly flocking to David to make him their King. And that verse is so powerful. It says that the men of Issachar understood the times and knew what Israel should do.

In other words, God's people at that time understood what was happening to them and they knew exactly what they had to do. They knew that a time of change had come and in the earth things are constantly changing, seasons and years.

The earth is constantly changing. We go out one week and we see new growth and new trees, new plants, new flowers, new dawns, new sunsets, new skies. Everything is constantly changing in the earth and even society itself is changing. We see that the governments change, the people change, the trends, the fashions, everything is changing. If you look at the fashions and study the fashions since the beginning of this century, the 1900s all the way up, you see how the style of dress has changed, how the attitudes have changed, how everything about this society and this world has totally changed.

And many times we think, well is change a good thing? Sometimes it is, sometimes it isn't, but we have to realize that if we want to reach this generation we have to change too, that the Church has to change its outlook. And we have to change how we view society.

I want to read something from John Wesley's *Journal* which he wrote on Sunday, 20 May 1759. Wesley, as you know, was the field preacher. He used to go out into the villages and the towns. Whenever the preachers used to go to the towns in those days, because of the way society was – there wasn't much news or information that ever got to the villages or the towns -- as soon as a preacher came to town the whole of the village would go out to listen to him. Wesley talks in his

Journal of often having crowds of ten to twenty thousand people standing in front of him listening to the Gospel.

Wesley and [George] Whitefield reached millions of people. They knew what was the right time for their generation, they knew that field preaching – getting out of the churches, getting to where the people were – they knew that that was the right thing for their generation, to be able to reach their generation, and they upset many of the established institutions for doing it during their day. But they understood that to reach the human need, which there was, they had to go against the institutions and do what they knew God was telling them to do, which was to get out and do the field preaching. Wesley says: 'I preached at eight in an open place at The Gins, a village on one side of the town. Many were there who never did and never would come to the room.'

He was talking about people who were there who would never go into a church, but they would come to listen to him preach. And he says: 'Oh, what a victory Satan would gain if he could put an end to field preaching, but that I trust he never will, at least not until my head is laid.'

And Wesley was right there. Satan didn't put an end to field preaching until the end of Wesley's days, and today we see that field preaching has stopped. If a preacher comes to a village, if I was to go onto the village green and say: 'Right, knock on every house door and say "A preacher has come to the village green to preach"', you would probably get two or three people out, four people out. Most of the people wouldn't be interested in coming out to listen to a preacher preach in the open air today.

It's a different time and a different society, and we live in a time when society has so much information – this generation more than any other generation who has ever walked the earth – this generation has more information and more technology available to it than any other generation on this earth. You know they have television, they have computers, they have newspapers, they have magazines, you can put on the television, and you can watch a foreign country, see wildlife you'd never have dreamed of seeing a hundred years ago. You can sit in your front room and you can see all the nations of the world, and programmes which explain and teach about these things. There's so much information that if a preacher comes to a village nowadays with the message of the Gospel, the people are getting so much information that they think it's no big deal. We are getting so much information:

why do we want to listen to what a preacher says?

Because of that, masses, masses and thousands of people are going without hearing the Gospel of Jesus Christ. If we go and knock on the door we say to them 'Hi, I'm so-and-so', and try talking to them about the Lord or invite them to the church. They may listen for a minute or so and say 'Well thank you very much for your time', and then close the door. Or you may go up to them and talk to them on the street and they'll give you about a minute-and-a-half, or two minutes if that. You put something through the door. They may read it then they'll screw it up and put it in the bin.

You invite them to church and they say: 'Well, what's church got for me?' A well-known TV presenter recently said 'Church is the most boring experience there is in Britain.' And this is a well-known TV presenter; and when you look at the way society is, there is so much entertainment, there's so much information, there's so much to do out there that to actually invite people to church, a lot of the time they think, 'Well, what's church got for us?'

Often they are right. Some churches you go into can be boring. People can sit through the service and they can be bored throughout the service. And I think the message which God is saying to the generation at this time is that when the Christian Church is through changing, then we're through. The Church has to learn to change with the times. We have to make church attractive, so that people want to come to church.

I personally believe that the one way to reach this generation is through television; through having preachers on the television who can preach the truth. But that seems far in the distance, that doesn't seem to be happening yet. So to get the people to come to listen to what we have to say, to the Gospel, we have to make the church attractive. The young generation has to have something which is attractive in the service. I was reading a book and this preacher said that the duty of the Church is to entertain the people when they come. And I sat there and I thought 'No, that's not right'. And then I carried on reading and he started talking about the actual word 'entertainment'. He says many people think the word 'entertainment' is to put on a show or to have fun. And he said the actual word 'entertain' means, to hold the attention of. That when people come into the church you hold their attention, that when the young people come into the church their attention is gripped by what is happening in the service.

That is what we need to do to be able to get the young people. We need to be able to have the sort of services where they come in and say 'I like this, I can relate to this.' Then they'll listen to what we have to say. But if they come into a service and it's not relevant to them or it's not touching their age group, then they're going to think 'Well, we're not going to come back again, this is boring.'

The men of Issachar understood the times, and we as Christians need to understand the times today. A pastor said 'If you are getting the job done, I like the way you are doing it.' Effectiveness is always more important than tradition. Always more important than tradition, and when we talk about change we are not talking about changing the teaching or the doctrine of the Church, but we are talking about changing the presentation of the Church.

It says here, I've written, the people who have been born in the twentieth century have witnessed more change in their daily lives and the world about them than anyone else who has ever walked the earth. And yet many times as Christians and churches we think that we can't change, we want to be relics of a medieval age which is not relevant to the young people today. It disturbs and distresses me greatly to think that thousands and thousands of young people have never been into church. I mean people twenty or thirty years old. The only times they may go into church is for a funeral or for baptism or a wedding or something like that, but they are never going to a church and they are not hearing the Gospel and it's like the old song:

> Humpty Dumpty sat on a wall,
> Humpty Dumpty had a great fall,
> All the king's horses and all the king's men,
> Couldn't put Humpty together again.

Society has had a fall, society has fallen out there and all the kings' horses, the governments, are trying to put it back together, but they won't be able to. Because only God can do that. Only God can put society back together. And God's instrument for working with society is the Church, the Christian Church. We're supposed to be the body of Christ to work in this generation and in the early Church you see the needs of the hour always dictated the nature of ministry.

It was the same with Christ. The need of the hour always dictated the nature of ministry – not the traditions, but the needs of the hour. We looked last week at the man with the shrivelled hand: when he came into the church, the Pharisees, with all their tradition and their religion, they looked to see if Christ would heal this man on the Sabbath. And Jesus said to them, 'What is lawful? Is it lawful to do good on the Sabbath or to do evil?' And they wouldn't answer him. So he said to the man, 'Stretch out your hand', and as the man stretched out his hand it was totally healed.

You know that the need dictated how Christ had the ministry, and that's how we've got to be, so that human need always dictates how we have ministry and human need always dictates how we have church. If people come in here and you can see that they are convicted by the Holy Spirit after the first song, we stop the worship service, we preach the Gospel to them, we proclaim the Gospel to them. Some people would say, well, surely we should sing the second song, then the third hymn, then the fourth song, then go into the sermon, then have the last song. You know we can't set rigid rules with God. When the Holy Spirit starts moving we can't set rigid rules with God and think, right, we're going to have church this way. If people come in and people start getting healed in our services – and I've been in services where I've seen it happen – what are we going to do? Are we going to say 'God, wait until we've finished what we're doing, then please come and move amongst us with your power?'

We can't do that. As soon as the Holy Spirit starts moving and starts touching people's lives, then the ministry, the way we have church, has to change to flow with what God's doing. Just as we sang, 'Do not strive, do not strive', we have to submit and yield to the Holy Spirit.

Jesus said:

> 'You are the ones who justify yourselves in the eyes of men, but God knows your hearts. What is highly valued among men is detestable in God's sight.'
>
> [Luke 16:15 NIV]

What is detestable in God's sight was the Pharisees when they had the traditions and the religion, and yet they were so blind and so shut out to human need. And Christ rebukes them fervently many times. He called them hypocrites, he called them broods of vipers, he called them all of these things because they had the tradition, yet they were so blind to human need that people would come into their synagogues hurting with the pains of life, and the people would come in, they'd be suffering, and their religious tradition would be blind to that suffering. Christ hated that and he still hates it today. The Church has to look to human need and that always has to dictate the nature of ministry.

Christ said:

> 'Woe to you teachers of the law and Pharisees, you hypocrites! You are like white washed tombs, which look beautiful on the outside but on the inside are full of dead men's bones and everything unclean.'
>
> [Matthew 23:27-28 NIV]

Every church should not just be a respectable institution. Every church should be a spiritual hospital for people's spiritual needs, that people can come into a church and have their needs met, whether it's a spiritual hurt, whether it's an emotional hurt or whether it's a physical hurt. They can come into a church and they can have that need met by God. God through us can reach that person with a need, whether it's something we sing or something we preach or whether we pray for that person. God, through us, wants to touch that person. We are Christ's hand on the earth, we are Christ's mouth on the earth, we are his eyes on the earth, so that Christ works on the earth through us, through the Church.

The Bible says that we are fellow workers with God, that we work together with the Holy Spirit. That when the Holy Spirit starts working we work together with him, we submit to him because he is our Lord. We yield and surrender to him, submit to him.

In Acts 10:37, with Peter and Cornelius, Peter says

> You know what has happened throughout Judea, beginning in Galilee after the baptism that John preached – how God anointed Jesus of Nazareth with the Holy Spirit and power, and how he went around doing good and healing all who were under the power of the devil, because God was with him.
>
> [NIV]

Humanity is so precious to God that God left the very realms of heaven to come to earth in human form to be whipped and beaten and tortured and crucified on a cross to be able to meet human need. That is how God viewed human need. That is the extent of God's love, that

God himself was willing to do that, to be able to meet the need there is in a hurting world. After three days he was resurrected and went to heaven and then he came back and spoke to his Apostles and he says to them, he says: 'You are my witnesses in the earth.' And he told the Apostles to wait for the power of the Holy Spirit and the presence of the Holy Spirit. When the Holy Spirit came the Church was so transformed that the power which Christ had, through the Holy Spirit, was given to the Apostles, and the Bible says that they went around healing people, they went around touching lives and helping people.

You know, the Holy Spirit has never left the earth. The Holy Spirit is still here amongst the Church. But many times throughout the history of the Christian Church, door after door has been shut to the Holy Spirit until we have, as it says in Second Timothy 3:5, that in the last days men will have a form of religion which denies the power. It will have the traditions of religion without the power and the presence of God amongst us, without the reality of Christ amongst us which is what we have to have, because that's so important to God that we do that.

The men of Issachar understood the times. And we as Christians today, we have to understand the times. We have to, as we saw last week, not be like the priest in the parable of the Good Samaritan who was so wrapped up in religious piety and tradition that he could leave a dying man bleeding in the gutter. As Christians we have to be able to meet human need first and that's got to always be the priority, that we meet human needs and that as a church we touch this village. And if we don't, as a church, touch this village and the surrounding area, then I believe we have failed the commission of Christ. The Bible teaches us in the parable of the Sower that our task is to be a witness and to proclaim the message and it talks about the four different hearers you get in the Gospel, the four different hearers and the four different responses you get to the Gospel. If people reject the Gospel, then we have done our duty before God, because if they have heard the Gospel and they reject it we have done our duty in fulfilling the commission and there is nothing we can do for those people apart from pray for them. But we have to understand that we have to flow with the times, we have to understand what is happening in our generation and get the ministry of the Church to meet that need, not to satisfy our own traditions or our own way which we have church, because Christ is coming again, and I believe that before Christ comes again the Church is going to go through a mighty and a powerful revival which will touch the lives of many people – and this is happening in various countries of the world at the moment.

We need to pray that that will happen here in Britain too, that God will start to move as he did in the days of the Bible and that God will start to move as he has in the times of revival in the history of the Church. The Bible says that Jesus Christ is the same yesterday, today and forever, so Christ never changes, his ministry never changes, and yet his vessel through which he is working on the earth at the moment is us, the Church. So let us pray:

> Heavenly Father, we long to be the sort of Church which I have just spoken about, God: the Church which is your living and moving and working body in this earth, so that you touch people through us, you touch people as we speak and Lord God, so that all of human need may be met, so that anybody who comes into the church, whatever need they have, that, Lord God, they will find the answer in your word which is explained there and that every person who comes into this church, Lord, who has hurts or anything – Lord, we are weak humans, Lord, and as servants we may fail you many times, Lord God, in our ministries, but as children we thank you that your love remains the same for us, Lord, and we pray that when people come in, Holy Spirit, that you meet them and that you would touch their lives and that your conviction, that your conviction may come upon them so powerfully, Lord, that their lives may be changed and their lives may never be the same again. We thank you for this, Father, in Jesus's name. Amen.

Obey the State Authorities

Sermon preached by William Alford at Abbey Street Methodist Church, Armagh, on 11 September 1994.

Mr Alford, 67, married with three sons and a banker with the Royal Bank of Ireland for 14 years until he was ordained in 1963, believes 'that when one is called into the full-time ministry it is very much a preaching ministry, a ministry of proclamation. Preaching can encourage people who sit under the word to go out with a new sense of purpose and direction. I also believe that preaching can encourage people to have a look at themselves if what is being said is related to everyday life. I do believe change doesn't come from the preacher, but God uses the preacher as his instrument to encourage people to change.'

Bible texts: Isaiah 45:1-7; Romans 13:1-7; Matthew 22:15-22

Everyone must obey the state authorities

The apostle Paul was conscious of the dangers and pitfalls which faced the Christian disciple who was a citizen of two worlds – the temporal and the eternal. One had to be so careful that Christian liberty did not deteriorate into licence when it came to observing the laws of the state. Rebellion against lawfully constituted authority ended with the death penalty and no one was exempt. It was therefore of the utmost necessity to warn the Christian community to observe strictly the rule of law and on no account ever to attempt civil disobedience. If the law were to be challenged, let it be challenged through the proper channels in the system.

St Paul is counselling obedience to the state authorities, not merely for the sake of avoiding punishment. He is doing something much more positive – namely, encouraging the Christian community to set an example in good citizenship – that high standard of citizenship which arises out of the nature of organized society reflects the higher fulfilment of God's purpose for man's eternal good.

So, in verse 1 he says: 'Let every person be subject to the state authorities' – everyone – religious leaders, political leaders, captains of industry – no one is above the law. This needed to be stressed since there were many within his congregations who would rather claim immunity from the state than accept the full responsibility of citizenship. In Paul's mind all authority ultimately rests with God. This is not to assume that all authorities are just, or that all governments are above reproach, but it does imply that behind all human activity there is the providential ordering of the world. Order in human society is God's provision for safeguarding lives. St Paul, in recognizing the fairness and impartiality of the Roman legal system, saw that system as a reflection of the divine order, since all authority comes from God. Therefore he maintained that those who broke the law flouted the authority of God.

In verse 2 we have the phrase 'he who resists the authorities', placing the emphasis upon the individual. The Apostle is focusing his attention on the selfish kind of individualism which undermines community values and endangers the lives of others. This sort of irresponsibility which put one's own opinions above the common good did little to commend the Gospel.

It is worth recalling the fact that there were Christians living within the shadow of Caesar's palace who realized only too well what the writer meant by the words, 'he who resists will incur judgement'...a warning to all who in their enthusiasm for reform needed to be reminded of the inevitable consequences of their actions. The advice of our Lord to his followers applied at all times – 'be as wise as the serpent and as harmless as the dove'.

In verse 3 we are told that the law-abiding citizen who respects the law need have no fear of it, and that those who do what is right need not fear the authorities; on the contrary, he will receive their commendation: sound government gives positive encouragement to the good citizen.

In verses 4 and 5 St Paul enunciates his firm belief that behind the organized affairs of state there was the moral order. This moral order signified a higher authority in which the magistrate was God's agent in the administration of justice. Therefore the person who does what is right will find the administrator of justice to be God's agent for good. On the other hand the perpetrator of mischief will find the same administrator to be God's instrument of retribution. St Paul would not have agreed with those who took the state benefits but did not respect its flag and anthem. Loyal and responsible citizenship meant living on a higher plane, and for the Christian that meant seeing the state as firmly placed in the natural order of things with distinct relevance to God's good purpose for the good of all.

In verse 6 there is a word for the income tax evaders. Cheating the state authorities harms everybody and has no place in the Christian way of life. Paying one's dues to the Inland Revenue, irrespective of one's religious persuasion or political outlook, is a way of honouring God, since the state is a part of the divine dispensation. To cheat the Inland Revenue therefore is not clever, it is dishonourable. Here again is the recurring theme of doing everything as unto God no matter who is in government.

Respect and honour, says verse 7, are the twin badges of the good citizen...respect for authority and honour toward all men. Patriotism of itself is not enough. It has little or no meaning if it is not reflected in responsible attitudes. 'Everyone must obey the state authorities.' Men and women from both sides of the religious and political divide are earnestly hoping for a successful outcome to the peace process in this our land. Much diplomacy and great patience will be needed before a satisfactory formula can be reached. Past wrongs will have to be acknowledged in the spirit of repentance, acceptance and forgiveness. Above all else, there will have to be a deeper awareness on all sides as to the duties and responsibilities of citizenship that will put an end, once and for all time, to the godfathers of greed and the perpetrators of violence and corruption. The language of bigotry and discrimination will be foreign to relationships.

St Paul would tell us, as he told the Christians in Rome, that this is all possible when a people's heart and mind are centred on the will of God as revealed in his Word and supremely demonstrated in the life and teaching of our Lord. He would contend that a Christian people will produce a government and a system that reflects the divine provision for man's good, upholding the right and condemning the evil in society. It is to this end that he urges everyone to accept the role of citizen in the spirit of willing service to the community, with a deep respect for authority...a respect born out of personal experience of the kingship of Christ and a love for one's neighbour.

The encouraging and challenging note with which Paul would finish is that this new era of peace, reconciliation and sound government begins with you and me, as by example we encourage all our brothers and sisters to love the Lord and obey the state authorities. Through the gift of the Holy Spirit, God will give us the grace and courage to extend his Kingdom so that we may go from here with a broader vision and a deeper commitment.

Amen.

Marriage at Cana

Sermon preached by Ian Knox at St John the Baptist, Westwood, Coventry, on 22 January 1995.

Ian is married with four sons and is a solicitor by profession. He has been a lay reader since 1968 in the Church of England and now works full time for the 40:3 Trust, a Coventry-based evangelistic organization which sends preachers around Britain and the world to teach and help people become Christians. Ian has visited Northern Ireland, Kenya, Niger and South Africa on behalf of the Trust. He became a Christian at the age of seven when he was standing in the doorway of Woolworths and a girl in the Salvation Army said: 'You need Jesus to be your saviour.' He decided quietly to trust Jesus, and as a lawyer found Christianity is provable, and therefore real. Last year he had two books published. Bereaved *(Kingsway) on bereavement, and* And All the Children Said Amen *(Scripture Union) on families and praying together. Ian says 'The good news of Jesus is the best news in the world. The tragedy so often is that we don't tell people in the right way so they don't hear and don't have a chance to respond. People have a right to say no to Jesus, but if we don't give them the chance to say yes, how can they decide? We need to effectively communicate the Gospel in today's language to today's people.'*

Bible text: John 2:1-11

Let's give God a chance this morning and ask him to speak to us as we pray words together that say, Lord Jesus Christ please speak to me. Let's pray that together.

Lord Jesus Christ, please speak to me. Amen.

As a decent church-going Anglican, don't you think many Christians go slightly OTT – over the top? It's all right for people taking part in the National Lottery – please don't own up to it here that you've got a ticket – we just have numbers in our house, we don't buy tickets, we amuse ourselves to see how few numbers we've got. My wife's maximum I think has been two, but I can't remember which week that was. But it's all right to get excited about winning £8.5 million. It's all right to get excited when somebody called Andy Cole plays for Manchester United. It's all right to get worked up, to be at least vaguely in love before you get married. But for somebody to say 'Praise the Lord' is obviously, seriously over the top.

So why is it that Christians feel that they have the right to be like that and to go even more over the top than anybody else? The answer is very simple. Because those of us who are Christians have found that Jesus Christ makes all the difference in the world to everything we are, and to everything we do, and to everywhere we go, and to our entire past, present and future. If anybody else in the world is allowed to be over the top for what they do, please forgive us when occasionally we go slightly over the top: because we think what we've got is a great deal better than what anybody else has got. And we want everybody else to have it as well – because being a Christian is the best thing you ever can be, and to become a Christian is the best thing you ever can do. And Jesus, from the very beginning of his ministry sought to show that he made all the difference in the world, and that difference was for the very best.

Looking at our reading from John 2, we see how God in Jesus gets involved in our world, and how Jesus does make all the difference. It's a marvellous scene. All those of us who've ever felt that we've wanted more help than we can give ourselves at home, feel this passage was written for us. Here is a wedding and Jesus is invited – what a brilliant thing to do. I don't know if you've ever been one of those people who has had the great joy of inviting the Lord Jesus to share in your home and your life, whether you've married or not, but that's what this young couple wanted to do. They wanted Jesus to be around and they invited him.

But when he came, they realized that they hadn't quite got it right. In the older translations, instead of 'when the wine was gone', in verse 3, it says 'the wine failed', which is rather splendid. I always feel it is slightly unfair on the wine, because the wine didn't even know it was being examined, never mind failed, and when it says 'the wine failed', you feel, well, that's rather sad for the poor wine because, actually, the fault lay not with the wine but the people who ordered it. They planned their wedding to be the very best, to be wonderful, to be marvellous, and then it all went wrong. The very thing that was there to make the wedding (forgive me for putting it like this) go with a sparkle – it just went. And they realized they hadn't got it right as they'd planned. They failed.

And I suppose that as we go along, we realize that's the way we get our lives, isn't it? – we plan our lives to be wonderful – we don't plan our lives as failures – we don't plan to get things wrong – we don't aim that we should make a mess of things – but in our own hearts and our own lives we know the truth is that we do get things wrong. Got it wrong again! And the strange thing is that, the older you get, you don't start getting your life more and more right. Your life actually carries on getting wrong, except you realize that your mistakes are more and more permanent, because you've less and less time to put them right. I can say that, as somebody who's going white and therefore knows this. It's all right when you set out with your young children, but when your babies grow to the age of my children, you realize it's a bit late to try to change whatever you should have done with them when they were younger. And you're left with, unfortunately, your own mistakes as well as your own successes, whatever you do.

Well, what do you do when you get things wrong? As we all get things wrong. What do you do when you have to come to church and the man at the beginning of the service gets us to hear words that say 'The blood of Jesus Christ makes us clean from all sin', and then immediately invites us to confess our sins, and we all know we have to confess our sins because we've all got them. We all have to look into our hearts, and say: 'I haven't been the perfect person I wanted to be, never mind what God wanted me to be. I wanted to be better than I was.' What do you do? What did *they* do?

They went to somebody who they thought might have an answer, and that person was Mary, who was obviously a very wise lady. She said the most brilliant thing that I think almost anybody has ever said – something that rings down the years with such a 'that's the right answer'. The servants came to Mary and they said: 'We're in a mess, this whole thing's fallen apart, what are we going to do?' And she pointed to her son Jesus and said: 'Whatever he says to you, do it.' And I am so glad to hear those words, because I know that when there is nothing that I can do about what I get wrong, I know a man who can. Jesus has the answer when we have the questions. Jesus has the right way when we've found the wrong way. And so Mary points to Jesus and says: 'Do what he says.' So they go and ask Jesus, and they say: 'What shall we do?' And Jesus asks them to do something which from all human standpoints is completely crazy – something which is totally demanding of them, as well as of him. He is going to work an amazing miracle. And they are going to have to put absolute trust and confidence in him for him to do it.

He says: 'Look at those water jars you've been using to wash people's feet.' You know when you go out to the Mediterranean, they don't have puddles of water where the rain's been, they have dust everywhere, because there hasn't been any rain. And when you walk along in your sandals, you get your feet dusty and sweaty and horrible. So at the door of the house you have these enormous jars of water, and they take a ladle of water from a jar and pour it over the people's feet. So they had these jars of water and Jesus said: 'I want you to go and take from those jars a cup of water. Take it to the person in charge of the feast, and you'll have your wine.'

Now it's easy for us 2,000 years later to look back over history and say obviously it was going to be wine. Anyone who rises from the dead can make water turn into wine, which is OK if he's risen from the dead, but not OK if he hasn't even died. It's easy to say, somebody who can stand at the grave of Lazarus and say 'Come out', and Lazarus comes out, can easily turn water into wine. But he hasn't done *that* yet. It's easy to say that somebody who can feed 5,000 people with five loaves and two fish can easily turn a drop of water into a drop of wine. But he hasn't fed 5,000 people yet. He hasn't done any miracles.

This is the very first one. What he's asking these servants to do is something totally new to them. It is complete commitment to somebody they've never seen do anything – somebody they've never trusted before. And they put their entire lives on the line to do it. Because what's going to happen is they're going to take this water and they're going to go up to the man in charge of the feast, and they're going to say: 'Here you are, here's the w——, here you are.' And he is then going to take it and say: 'Thank you very much.' You know how they do it on the *Food and Drink* programme: 'Lake Galilee, AD 30 – it was a very good year for water.' And he's then going to say 'Listen, this *is* water. What sort of idiot joke is this? What sort of fool do you take me for? Get out, you're not paid for this job, you're sacked, and because we live in this small town of Cana I'll see you never work in this area again.'

Do you see the danger of what they're doing? They're putting their entire lives on the line – to trust this person they've never trusted before – whom they've never seen do anything wonderful before – they are trusting in the most total way. And I don't want to kid you on. I do believe that when somebody like me asks people to step into becoming Christians I'm asking them to do a very very hard thing. It's easier if you've been a Christian a number of years to trust Jesus again. In some ways it's always hard to trust Jesus because you're trusting him for new things, even if you've been a Christian for many years. It must be easier to trust him again, once you've trusted him a number of times. But if you have never trusted him, you are being asked to do something that is very tough.

And it was no small thing for those servants, because we are not actually talking about a drop of water being changed into a drop of wine. When you look at the quantity stated here in John 2, half a dozen jars, each containing 20 or 30 gallons, it rolls off the tongue easily, but you'd be arrested at Dover for bringing them in. We're not talking about going to Safeways and buying a couple, we're talking about 1,000 bottles of wine. This is going to keep Cana afloat for weeks! And they take this wine to the man – and it *is* wine. The person who needs to be convinced most finds that's what it is. It isn't water that tastes like wine – it's wine. And it is the *best* wine. He admits it. In fact he actually makes a joke of it by saying: 'We always serve the best wine first because people's taste buds are in good shape at the beginning, but later on, when they've had a few, they can't tell the difference. So we give them the cheap plonk after that. And what have you done? You've saved the best wine until now. What a funny thing to do.' And those of us who trust Jesus make this amazing discovery: that he is the One who, however excellent things have been up until now, changes them as if they were just like water becoming wine. He makes even the best seem commonplace compared with what he is able to give to us.

There's an idea around that the only people who ever become Christians are people whose lives have fallen into the gutter, and somehow they need dragging out, because that's the only way they'll ever stand up again. Now I thank God that he does rescue people from the gutter, and he does change lives which are in a terrible, serious mess. But I am equally glad that he is someone who changes lives which are OK into lives which are transformed by the new life he gives. I dare to tell you this morning, you may be the most successful person who has come to church today, but if you do not have Jesus, he will make all the difference in the world to you if you trust him; as well as to the worst person who's come to church who needs as much help as they can get. And why is that? It is for two very special reasons.

I do not believe that it is a coincidence that the first miracle Jesus ever wrought involved water and wine, because three years later he took another cup which did have wine in it, and said: 'This is my blood which is shed for you – drink this all of you.' It was that amazing picture of the blood he was going to shed the following morning, when they would take him out and put him on that cross where the blood of Jesus Christ would make us clean from all sin. Every one of us needs the wonder of our lives changed by Jesus, and the sign of that wonder is the shed blood of Jesus as he comes to wash away all our sins. Even the nicest, most successful, most wonderful person in church this morning needs that to happen, and Jesus comes to wash us clean with the wine of his blood.

And he also used the other picture of the water. Later in John's Gospel, Jesus is going to stand up at one of the great feast days in Jerusalem, and is going to say: 'If anyone is thirsty, let him come to me and drink', which he said of the Holy Spirit. In Acts 2, the Holy Spirit was sent upon the disciples, and with that fullness of his Spirit he can transform our lives today. He changes our lives with the wine of his blood and the water of his Spirit.

People talk a great deal these days of signs and wonders, and I thank God for the wonderful things that are happening in our land and in our world, but the greatest sign and wonder is when an old life is changed into a new life, when a dead life is changed into a living life, when a life that is heading for a lost eternity becomes a life which is heading for heaven. And Jesus Christ this morning comes to us, and he says: 'I want to change the water of your life into the wine of the Kingdom of Heaven.'

Whoever else you hear saying 'I can help you with your life', and thank God, there are many who do, there is no one who will help us with our lives like Jesus. Nobody will make the wonderful difference that only he can make, and I long this morning that every last one of us in church may give him the chance as we take courage in both hands, and we take that water of our lives and we say: 'I've never really let you, Jesus, make this miracle happen. Change me, change my life into the wine of your Kingdom.' There is a marvellous verse, written 3,000 years ago, when the Psalmist says this: 'Oh taste and see that the Lord is good' [Psalm 34:8].

Dear friends, this morning may every last one of us drink deeply of God and know that our lives will never be the same because he has made them new. Jesus didn't go to that wedding to make it boring. He didn't go to that wedding to turn them off God. He went to that wedding to be with them and to bless them and give them the best. And when they had the nerve to let him, they found that's what happened. And here today, you're perhaps sitting there thinking: 'I need that transforming work of God's presence in my life. Come and change me. Come and fill me with the wine of your love; with the water of your power. Come and make me new. Lord Jesus, do it.'

If God has spoken to your heart this morning, and I do believe for many of us he's touched us and said, 'Let me bring my blessing to you: let me bring my change to you', then say one word to the Lord Jesus. The word 'Yes'. Let's be quiet in prayer, as you do.

Jesus and Evil Spirits

Sermon preached by Trevor Mapstone at St Thomas's, Penny St, Lancaster, on 12 February 1995.

Trevor, 32, married with two children, was ordained in 1989, did two years as a volunteer parish worker in a church on Merseyside before being accepted for the ministry and training at St John's, Nottingham. He is currently doing an MA in Religious Studies at Lancaster, focusing on the charismatic movement in the Church of England. St Thomas's, where he is the curate, has a regular worshipping congregation of 400, of all ages but with many students. It is a prime example of how the established church has embraced charismatic evangelicalism within its fold. Trevor says: 'Preaching is important because the Bible is important and the Bible needs to be applied. That is what preaching aims to do. It does this by being faithful to the original message, believing it has relevance for today and finding points of contact with people's experience.'

Bible text: Mark 5:1-20

A lady was trying to explain to her little boy of four what it meant to become a Christian and so she decided to use the picture of Jesus, *The Light of the World*, which Holman Hunt had painted; the very well-known picture based on Revelation 3:20 which talks of Jesus standing at the door and knocking. And so she showed this to her son and said to him: 'Jesus is knocking at the door of your heart, what are you going to say to him?' And he said: 'By the hair on my chinny chin chin, you can't come in!'

That story says a lot about how you can convey the faith to children and also about abusing Bible texts to do evangelism, but I've used it today because our story in Mark's Gospel is about people not wanting to let Jesus in and it also involves pigs!

Two weeks ago we had a sermon on Jesus and evil spirits and this is really part two. The first account was in Mark 3 where we read of an encounter between Jesus and the Pharisees when they accused him of being possessed by demons. He explained to them how he was the one who could set people free from the devil, far from being possessed by the devil. Today we see that in action; we see Jesus fulfilling his own words in actually setting someone free from the power of evil, and I want to look at this story from two angles.

The first thing that it shows us is about the power of Jesus to set us free from evil. This man was so overwhelmed with evil and so wild with evil that nobody could do anything for him and so he was out in the tombs outside the town. The first thing we notice about Jesus' power to help him is that there is nowhere that is out of bounds for Jesus. Nowhere is out of bounds. Everything about this incident between Jesus and the demon-possessed man would suggest that Jesus had no business doing what he did, where he did it. From a Jewish point of view, everything about this place was unclean. It was in Gentile territory on the other side of Galilee. Geraza was a city about 35 miles south east of Galilee. The man lived in the tombs, an unclean place, and he was possessed by evil spirits, the pig is an unclean animal as far as Jewish law goes, so everything about it would suggest that Jesus the Jew had no business there and that the God of the Jews had nothing to do with that area. It was religiously very different and yet Jesus is able to manifest the power of God there. In an alien place, Jesus' healing and power is just as strong as it is in the synagogue, in any place where the God of the Jews would be acknowledged and worshipped. Jesus is able, even in this alien place, to do what he wants to do, and this is very significant for us because we might think that there are certain areas of life where Jesus' power is not influential, where Jesus is unable to have any influence, where Jesus is weak.

We may feel that Jesus' power is restricted to the Church, to our religious activities, that Jesus has power to do certain things in certain instances, but not outside of those instances. When it comes to things like where we work, when it comes to the realm of politics, when it comes to the arts and the media and science and economics, we have a very difficult job in thinking that Jesus is just as powerful there as he is now, as he is when we are praying for people, when we're ministering to people. We may feel that Jesus is unable to stand against the tide of indifference and apathy that people have towards him and so we feel frightened to go out into those places and to expect Jesus to be Lord there. That is, in a sense, a temptation for us. We may not be conscious of it, but, from time to time, we feel it, when we feel afraid of being a Christian in those places, or even of praying for those areas of life. And here in Mark 5, you couldn't get a more anti-Jesus place than the site of these tombs outside this town. And what happens here is that Jesus is fully able to demonstrate his power and his lordship and he can do that in any area. We might be frightened that Jesus can't come up with the goods in certain areas of public life, that Christianity only works in private, that it's about saving my soul from sin, healing my inner hurts, and that's as far as it goes. We secretly believe that Jesus has no power really to affect society. How sad for my private life and this Church; as if out of church he'd be like Samson without his hair – useless and weak – and we'll be left defeated and our faith will be shown to be stupid and we'll feel humiliated. There's a great danger in our society for us to feel that way because we are in a minority and it seems that the vast majority of people out there are anti-Jesus, and we can be tempted to think that he has no power there. But if we do think that then we're actually denying that Jesus is Lord. He's not just Lord of me, he's Lord of all. He's Lord of every area of life. In every area he can demonstrate his power and he shows here, by delivering this demon-possessed man, by setting him free in a foreign, unclean and alien place, that he is Lord.

And that means for us that if we believe in Jesus and we take Jesus with us, then we can be bold. Maybe in our studies, if we're having to read things and take on board ideas which we know are anti-Christ, and anti-God, we don't need to be afraid, we can take those things on. We can explore those things because we know that Jesus is Lord, and we don't need to be frightened for him. It means we can apply our Christianity to our work and expect Jesus to have an influence there. It means that we don't need to be afraid to get involved in things as a Church, in the arts – like the Artshouse – we're moving into territory which perhaps some Christians feel Christians have no business in, but Jesus is Lord of that. We may want to move into areas of social care and justice in this city. Jesus is Lord of that too and we are quite at liberty to take him into those areas and to exercise power in his name in those areas. So, nowhere is out of bounds for Jesus and we can be confident of that.

The second thing about his power is that nothing is too difficult for him. If you look at verse 3, it says that this man lived in the tombs and no one could bind him any more, not even with chains. No one was strong enough to subdue him. And when Jesus asks him what his name is, he says 'My name is Legion'. Now a legion in a Roman army contains 3,000 to 6,000 soldiers – that's the quantity of evil that was in this man. He was overrun by evil spirits, his personality was fragmented, his life was in pieces. There was nothing to be done for him – no one could bind him, he was totally out of control, and yet Jesus restores him and sets him free, and he binds the strong man, as he said he would do in Mark chapter 3. So there's no disorder, there's no situation either in our own lives or the lives of those we care for, or in the life of our Church, or the life of our society – there is no situation which is too difficult for him.

Now that might raise a question for us. If Jesus can do anything, if he can heal anything, if he can restore anyone, why doesn't he do that every time we pray for people? Why doesn't he heal everybody and restore everyone? Well, the answer is actually implied in this story. We can't control Jesus, we can't tell him what to do. In fact, in this story nobody asked him to do this. The opposite is true. They wanted him to go away. No one asked Jesus to heal the demon-possessed man. He was totally free and sovereign in this situation to do what he wanted to do. He takes the initiative and he does as he pleases. And that's hard for us to take because we want to feel that if we tell Jesus to do something, he'll do it. If we pray for someone to be healed, they'll be healed – but, unfortunately, it doesn't work like that. We have to just acknowledge that he is free and sovereign and knows what's best in each situation. He could cure all diseases and wipe out all evil at a stroke, but he chooses not to. He is totally free to do as he wishes with us and with this world and, in a sense, that should give us confidence because if he really was at our beck and call, then we'd be in trouble, but we can be sure that whatever Jesus does or doesn't do is for the ultimate purpose of advancing the Kingdom of God. We have a guarantee of that and that is the Resurrection. The fact that Jesus rose again is a guarantee to us that evil has been defeated and will be ultimately wiped out. So, nothing's out of bounds and there's nothing too difficult for Jesus to do.

Now, some people, when they read this story, take it as a blueprint for how we're supposed to deal with people who may be struggling with being possessed with evil spirits and they take various bits of the story. For example, some may say that when you pray for somebody to be set free from evil, you have to ask the evil spirits to name themselves before you can do that. But that's a very dangerous thing to do. For one thing, the devil is the 'father of lies' and you may never get the right answer. But, for another thing, it's a bit selective because no one ever suggests that you're supposed to have a herd of pigs kept in the vestry! You know, you take bits of the story, but not other bits. All we need to take from this instance about Jesus' power is that he is able to set people free, and whenever we're ministering to people, all we're doing is asking him to do his will and to bring his power. It's his job to heal people, to exorcise them of evil and we simply join in with what he's doing. We ask him and we seek him to come. We don't need to get involved with whatever evil is there. We simply say: 'Jesus come! We know that you've got the power. You do it.'

That's one angle that we can look at the story from. The other is the way people responded to Jesus in this story, and the first response that we find is *fear*. The demon-possessed man is terrified of Jesus, but, not only he and the demons – the crowd too. The people who see this going on are also afraid and that's surprising. Verse 15 says when they came to Jesus they saw the man who had been possessed by the legion of demons, sitting there, dressed and in his right mind. And they rejoiced, they thanked Jesus, they ran over and congratulated the man... Well, no, it doesn't say that, does it? It says they were afraid. You'd have expected those other responses but, actually, they were afraid, and it's a frightening thing when Jesus actually comes in power and people's lives start to be changed and things start to happen. It's frightening. And it's often only when people's lives begin to show changes, and their life-style changes and the way they relate to people changes, that they begin to encounter opposition as a Christian. It's OK to believe in Jesus as long as that doesn't really make too much difference, but when it starts to affect things and you become obviously different and people start to get uncomfortable, if you let it affect your priorities and the decisions that you make, then people start to feel slightly uncomfortable with you.

A British journalist some time ago was writing about his son who'd been converted to Christ and become a Christian, and he saw this as the ultimate act of rebellion – worse than if his son had been on drugs or had lived a promiscuous life and slept with lots of people. It was the ultimate insult to the family for this person to turn to Christ and become a Christian and allow that to affect his life. It disturbs people that Jesus makes a difference. It's frightening, and so it should be.

These people – before Jesus came, they knew how things stood. Everything was sorted. The demon-possessed man was over there in the tombs and they were able to live their lives as best they could, as normally as possible. Life was stable. But now, here's Jesus upsetting the applecart and who knows what he's going to do next. If he can change this man, well, he might change me. He might come and start sorting us out as well, and there's no way we're going to let that happen! So, they were afraid. And it's not just non-Christians who feel like this. We too can feel this way. Our situation may not be ideal but we may have come to a place where we can cope with it as the townspeople did. There may be areas of pain and hurt, there may be areas of sin and bitterness, but we get to the stage where we feel we can cope. It's in its place, it's there and we live with it, just as they lived with the demon-possessed man. We can cope with it without dealing with it – in our inner life, in a particular relationship, in the Church, in the home. It's there, but we're living with it, it's OK, we're functioning. The whole area is spiritually wrong, but we've learnt how to live that way and tolerate it, and we can be tempted to keep Jesus out because to let him in to deal with that will be frightening.

You can picture it in terms of a house: your life as a house. And there are some rooms in your house where you will welcome guests and you will be happy for them to come in and sit down and enjoy your company. There will be other places in your house where you will not want them to go. My wife hates it when people come into the kitchen if we've got people round for a meal. She just hates having people there while she's cooking! There may be places in your life, areas in your life, where you're unable to let Jesus into, that you shut him out of. Other bits you're happy for Jesus to have control of, but there are some places where he's shut out. And that's what the townspeople were doing here. They were shutting him out. And, actually, they weren't that different from the demon-possessed man. They may have thought they were, but they were both on the same road. It's just that the demon-possessed man was further down the road. He had shut Jesus out completely – shut God out completely. They were shutting him out, a little bit, but they would have ended up in the same place. And what's going to be our fate if we keep Jesus out of certain parts of our life? We may need help in facing up to these things, in looking to allow Jesus in to those painful places, the places where we've shut Jesus out. We may need help to bring him in and let him do what he wants to do, difficult as that might be.

The second response is *resistance* and this is for a different reason. Verses 16 and 17: those who had seen it told the people what had happened to the demon-possessed man and told about the pigs as well and then the people began to want him to leave the region. Why did they want him to go? Yes, they were afraid of what he might do to them, but they were annoyed about the cost of all those pigs. Two thousand pigs don't come cheap! This had been expensive. OK, the man was restored to his right mind, but look at these pigs that have gone. It's ridiculous, it costs too much to have Jesus doing his will. There's a cost to calling Jesus 'Lord' and allowing him to do what he wants to do with us. It can be expensive. It may be expensive financially, but it could be expensive in other ways. It may cost us our pride, it may cost us in areas of career choice, in life-style choices, in sorting out relationships. It will cost us to let Jesus have his way and the cost may put us off as individuals and as a church. Some people are so put off by the cost that they will reject the healing and restoration because it costs too much – not prepared to pay the cost of moving forward with Jesus because it will cost too much. So, there's *fear* and *resistance* and the third response is *obedience*.

The man, in contrast to the people, having been restored and in his right mind, is prepared to obey Jesus. He was afraid of him. He was resistant to him, but Jesus had restored him and now all he wants is to go and be with Jesus, to be with this one who had set him free. You'd think that all the difficulty was behind him, that there could be nothing worse than his condition at the beginning of this story but, actually, the hardest was still to come. Jesus wouldn't let him come with him. Jesus said to him, 'Go home to your family and tell them how much the Lord has done for you.' Jesus is sending him away and he's sending him to people who have already shown that they don't want anything to do with Jesus. He's sending him to them to tell them what Jesus has done. It would have been far easier for him to have stayed with Jesus, in the company of those who were like-minded and who loved Jesus. That would have been a good place to be, but his healing wasn't just for his own benefit. He was restored so that he would then be able to go and be an ambassador for Christ. He was equipped now to share Jesus with others. And we may feel that Jesus is there to heal us, to restore us, to make us right and stay with that, and we want to stay in the company of those who are like-minded and who support us and love us and stay in the place where Jesus is ministering to us. But that's only half of the story. He only does that for us – and he does do that – but he only does it so that we may then be strong enough to go and to tell those in the alien places about him.

Mother Teresa said 'Evangelism means to carry Jesus in your heart and to give the presence of Jesus to someone else. They see God in us and we also see God in them, but to give Jesus to a person you must have Jesus yourself.' And what happens here is that this man is put in a position where he can now take Jesus to these people.

Whatever encouragement, healing, fellowship we may get from being in the Church, in a sense it's a means to an end. It's a means to the end of spreading his Kingdom. Jesus wants to use us to do that. It may be that he sends us back to our families. For some people that's the hardest place to share Jesus. My parents took twelve years to become Christians after I did; it's a long time of patient and not-so-faithful witness on my part! But it may be the workplace that Jesus is calling you to go to; it may be other places that he wants to send you to be his witness. The man has been healed so that he may then go with Christ to others. It's difficult because all we want to do really is enjoy Jesus and receive from Jesus, but he wants us to look outwards and to obey his call to go. 'Tell them how much the Lord has done for you and how he has had mercy on you.'

In our society the Church won't communicate Jesus as an institution. What communicates Jesus is people's lives which have been transformed by him. Being prepared to go and share that with others: that's what makes the difference and that's what happened with this man. The result – the man goes, he's obedient. In verse 20: 'The man went away and began to tell in the Decapolis how much Jesus had done for him and all the people were amazed.' That can be so for us.

The Sparrow and the Skylark

Sermon for Eastertide written by Donald Denman for Trumpington Parish Church, Cambridge.

Professor Denman has been a Reader in the Church of England for more than 30 years and was a former Member of the House of Laity of Church Assembly. Until recently Professor Denman, married with two sons and six grandchildren, preached regularly at Trumpington Parish Church, Cambridge and would have preached this sermon there had he not suddenly developed angina earlier this year and had to step out of the pulpit. The sermon was intended to address the difficulties of his age group, and he laments the lack of Christian literature for those over threescore years and ten. An identical twin, he has written many books, including his recently published autobiography, A Half and Half Affair: The Chronicles of a Hybrid Don *(Churchill Press), where he recounts his adventures in life, including his conversion in his early 20s. He says '"Go ye into all the world and preach the Gospel", is the Lord's command given as he left the earth on Ascension Day. That command still stands. Unfortunately the Church doesn't do over much about it.'*

In the year 627 at Godmundingham near York, Eadwine, pagan king of Northumbria, held a great assembly of nobles to hear Paulinus, chaplain to the Christian queen Aethelburga. One of the company expressed the feelings of all in the words:

> O king, often when men are sitting at meat in your hall a sparrow from the darkness flies in at one door, warms himself at the fire, and goes out of the opposite door. So it is with the life of man in this world; what has gone before it, what will come after it, no one can tell. If the strange teacher can say, let him be heard.

Paulinus rose to tell how man came from God the Creator and in Christ the Redeemer returns in him to life eternal.

That was fourteen hundred years ago. The allegory is still true today. We are all, as sparrows, flying from doorway to doorway through the world, and some of us are very near the outward door.

Is it dark or light outside? People today seldom ask the question, let alone seek an answer. Especially among western nations is it so. They have become too absorbed with the problems, prospects and prosperity of this world to bother about the next. Everything, the accumulation of experience, the accumulation of ideas, the accumulation of wealth, the accumulation of health must all be packed into this life. Death is a terminus, dark and funereal. Old age has nothing to offer but the ultimate deadline.

The Christian has always stood against the world. To this hopeless bathos, he is most vehemently opposed. St Paul's great struggle between 'natural man' and 'spiritual man' doesn't leave us at three score years and ten. Old age in a way intensifies the conflict. I write from experience and qualification: sixty years of spiritual struggle, a regiment of birthdays, eighty-three years long and a harlequinade of infirmities. By the world's standards, I'm a broken-winged sparrow.

The invidious influence of the world threatens spiritual hope. The spiritual battle never abates. The full armour of God is an ever necessary workaday adornment. For us sparrows the struggle can be likened to what the airlines call turbulence.

Christian confidence in Christ, risen to bring us eternal life, is the lodestar by which we steer. If the eyes of faith droop for a moment, the sparrow drops into a pocket of despair, doubt and gloom. There is no need to do so. 'My strength is made perfect in weakness' is the promise of the Lord to all ages. Over the weakness of old age with all its ills, the grace, power and presence of the Lord is intensified in proportion to need. Trust in him lifts the sparrow to a steady flight-path towards the light of eternal life beyond the doorway.

'We have received not the spirit of the world,' Paul reminds us, 'but the spirit which is of God; that we might know the things that are freely given to us of God.' The things Paul has in mind he had already referred to a few verses earlier in the second chapter of that first letter he was writing to the Corinthians:

Eye hath not seen, nor ear heard, neither have entered into
the heart of man, the things which God hath prepared for

them that love him.

[1 Corinthians 2:9 AV]

With that confidence in his heart, the Christian sparrow is on the flight-path to glory high above the turbulence. The exit door of life, when he reaches it, will become the very portal to Christ's Kingdom of glory.

Old age can be a time when the Holy Spirit manifests Christ in us with greater intensity than ever before, a time when each day is a doxology of praise, a spontaneous prayer of thankfulness. Christ's presence is so near, his promise so real.

In a recent obituary of Lady Ramsey, the widow of the Archbishop, the writer tells of her endearing impatience, ever more so after the Archbishop's death, for her *doxa*. This Greek word meaning glory should be a password for old age. It is also a word for springtime now upon us. Among the earliest flowers are the scillas whose bright blue faces herald the blue skies of summer. By their side in many gardens are close cousins, what the botanists call *chionodoxa*. In Greek, *chion* means snow and the end bit of the name is Lady Ramsey's *doxa*. English garden books know them as 'glory of the snow'. Let the chionodoxa in our gardens always remind us of the glory yet to be.

As the Christian sparrow flies through the outward doorway, he meets the spring morning of Christ's heaven and, a 'new creature' in Christ, soars high above a sparrow's flight, as a skylark.

Lord Hailsham enshrines this happy metaphor in the genius of the poem he wrote as an epilogue to his autobography, *The Sparrow's Flight*:

> Father, before this sparrow's earthly flight
> Ends in the darkness of a winter's night;
> Father, without whose word no sparrow falls,
> Hear this, Thy weary sparrow, when he calls.
> Mercy, not justice is his contrite prayer;
> Cancel his guilt, and drive away despair;
> Speak but the word, and make his spirit whole,
> Cleanse the dark places of his heart and soul,
> Speak but the word, and set his spirit free;
> Mercy, not justice, still his constant plea.
> So shall Thy sparrow, crumpled wings restored,
> Soar like a lark, and glorify his Lord.

Ministry and Service

Sermon preached by John Watson at Ivybridge Methodist Church, South Devon, on 23 July 1995.

Prebendary Watson, married with three children, was ordained in 1959 and was Church of England Vicar of St Andrew's, Plymouth until 1993. He served in the Army in Malaya during the Communist troubles and was promoted to Captain at the age of 19. He wrote a weekly religious 'Saturday Sermon' for The Western Morning News *for ten years and was a religious adviser to Independent Television for 20 years, but lost that job after a speech to the General Synod where he said there was not enough religious content in* Highway. *'Worship is the most important thing, and in order to enable people to worship and understand who they are worshipping, preaching is important. It is also an important evangelistic tool for the Church in reaching people outside it, through newspapers, television and also the Church, if you can get people into church. It is also important in shedding light on the textbook of the faith, the Bible.'*

Bible text: Isaiah 61:6

You will be known as…the servants of our God.

Tony Blair has recalled his followers to the perception of duty and service for which his party originally stood at a time when the balance of western affluence and Third World poverty is such that it is said the world cannot afford the USA, Japan and western Europe because we, 7 per cent of the world's population, consume 43 per cent of the world's resources, at a time when the every-man-for-himself attitude is threatening the structure of society, at a time of international unease when wars are proliferating and violence stalks the streets, at a time of breakdown of confidence in politics and politicians.

It was circumstances not dissimilar from these that originally brought Isaiah to God's house. In the midst of a domestic crisis and with the nation threatened by foreign powers we find him in the temple of God looking for a pattern of life which will make things come good, which will make life more as he senses God intends it to be. That interview with God ends with his going forth in the service of God, and here in a passage entitled 'The Good News of Deliverance' a keyword that springs to his mind is ministry, service.

Now I know this can be a pretty hackneyed word, but somehow in Isaiah's mind it had all the seeds of new life in it. God is moving massively on the political scene. There is to be good news for those humble enough to hear, new hope for those whose hearts have been broken, liberty for captives, release for prisoners, comfort for mourners, the rebuilding of a city, economic revival and the dawning of the Day of God. Thinking of service, Isaiah says: 'You shall be known as the servants of God.'

And when one thinks of outstanding examples of service down through the ages – Francis of Assisi, William Wilberforce, Mother Teresa – one realizes that this word isn't a meaningless word, it's really love in action.

Now in our generation we still have great necessities and aspirations, and service in many shapes and forms is necessary to meet them. Comprehensive need must be matched by comprehensive service. I was encouraged to hear a hospital administrator say the other day that more and more the importance of every member of the hospital team is being taken into account. It isn't just the supreme skills of the nurse and the physician and the surgeon – the cook and the consultant, the porter and the pathologist, the clerk and the cleaner all have a part to play in the total hospitality that is offered. (At last we in the Church are recognizing this, with every worshipper a worker, a greater collegiality, an every-member ministry...)

A comprehensive ministry: and many public and social services operate today to make life better and sounder and healthier. There's tremendous scope for Christians here, but so often the Church fails to play its part in combining with others to serve the needs of the inner personality, the soul, the whole man. Martin Luther King once said that the Christian must strive not only to do the work of the good Samaritan but also to make the whole road from Jerusalem to Jericho safe. Just so. Only by translating our doctrine into the structures of society will we gain attention for the Gospel we preach, by demonstrating that all the concerns of daily life are central and not marginal to the sphere of our responsibility. An enormous ministry.

We must not forget, however, that it is a humble ministry. But then true ministry always is. The very word ministry puts us in the role of servants because ministry means service. The holder of the greatest office in the land, oddly enough, is the first servant, the prime minister. I often think that the reason truly great people are truly humble is they realize the job they've got to do is so much greater than themselves and so wonderful in its effects that they don't worry about the dignity, they just get on with the job.

But you know as well as I do that we don't manage to live on that high plane for very long. A colleague of mine was once approached by an archbishop who asked, 'Who are you?' My friend replied, 'Oh, I'm just a humble curate.' Whereupon the archbishop exclaimed, 'Are you really? I didn't know there was such a thing!'

Yet the archbishop and the curate both know that the first thing that happens to every Anglican clergyman who's ever ordained is that he's made deacon, a word that comes from the Greek, *diakonos*, servant. And whatever he eventually becomes, he remains a deacon. And Jesus was a deacon. He came not to be served but to serve and to give his life a ransom for many. So the Christian is committed to the truth: Jesus gave his life for me and he lives his life in me. He served me to the end. I now serve him to the end and I realize that to do the work of the highest I must take the place of the lowest.

The secret of humble service lies in the well-expressed truth that man's humility does not begin with the giving of service, it begins with the readiness to receive it. A missioner approached a man at the bar of a pub and asked: 'If Jesus Christ were here, what would be the first thing he'd ask you to do for him?' With great insight the man replied: 'He wouldn't first ask me to do something for him, he'd first ask to do something for me.'

'You shall be named ministers of our God.' An enormous ministry with limitless possibilities. By definition a humble ministry. And thirdly and lastly, a glorious ministry.

Does not this passage in Isaiah demonstrate that ours is a regal religion, that there's great joy in service, that it's a glorious thing to serve? The year of the Lord's favour Isaiah wrote about was the year of Jubilee, when the sound of the silver trumpet swept over the hills and valleys. It proclaimed freedom, the restoration of man's inheritance and his place in God's plan. The destiny of man is surrounded with gladness and splendour if only we could realize it, and central to our calling, both here and hereafter, is the royalty of service, and this is something to be reflected in the character of all we offer to God. If you are to be named a minister then your bearing and disposition must support your claim to be his servant.

A Director of Stewardship recalled at a diocesan synod his father's witness and example. He was, he said, a poor, happy and humble man, a plumber. Every morning he would rise early, take breakfast with his large family and conduct family prayers with them. He would get up from the table and grasping his bag of tools with one hand and with his other on the handle of the door which led straight out into the street, he would then say:

> Forth in thy name, O Lord, I go,
> My daily labour to pursue,
> Thee, only thee, resolved to know
> In all I think, or speak, or do.
>
> [Charles Wesley, 1707-88]

Without another word or a backward glance, he would close the door behind him.

As the negro spiritual expresses it:

> Oh you gotta getta glory in the work you do,
> A hallelujah chorus in the heart of you.
> Paint or tell a story, sing or shovel coal,
> You gotta getta glory or the job lacks soul.

Yes, there's an attitude in service that can make the ordinary special. The plumber, whose joy in his work sprang from his faith in God, seemed to believe that the glory of God can be fully displayed in humble service. He would endorse the affirmation that nothing would bring nearer the promised day of God than that people should enter upon their profession in the spirit of those who regard it as their chief sphere of serving God.

'You shall be named the servants, the ministers of our God.' The true value of life is its content for others, and the greatest service you and I can render is that of enabling them to find fulfilment, as Jesus did; making weak people strong and sad people happy, as Jesus did; putting people in personal touch with God, as Jesus did; bringing to all we meet healing and comfort, light and liberty in the strength of him who died for us and rose again and in whose service is perfect freedom.

Just Beneath the Surface

Sermon preached by Bryan Coates at the Methodist Church, Chandler's Ford, Hampshire, on 24 July 1994.

Bryan Coates, 52, father of three sons, was ordained into the Methodist Church in 1970 at the age of 27. Bryan experienced a vocation to the ministry at 18 and he spent eight years in Africa, seconded to the United Church of Zambia. He says 'Preaching is a declaration of the truth and love of God in Jesus Christ. We haven't got all the answers but we attempt to relate God to people's lives and situations. Preachers try to have a foot in the world of God and a foot in the world of people's everyday experience, and to bridge the gap between those two worlds.' This sermon is the second in a series of three sermons, preached after the death of his wife Carol, as well as the church secretary Jocelyn Westmacott and pastoral lay assistant Marjorie Lowe, all from cancer, within the space of three months.

Bible text: Psalm 103:1,8

> Praise the Lord, my soul! All my being praise his holy name!..The Lord is merciful and loving, slow to become angry and full of constant love.
>
> [GNB]

Can I tell you, please, about Philip Kazhila, an African, a Zambian, a Lunda – one of the seventy or so tribal groupings that are lumped together in the present-day country of Zambia? The Lunda people occupy the territory in the far north-west corner of Zambia, and they stand testimony to the nonsense that was the division of Africa by Europeans at the tail-end of the last century. The Lunda people had an area of territory, and along came European map-makers and carved their area up, so that they found themselves in three different countries, dealing with three different nationalities from western Europe, and expatriates speaking three different languages. Part was designated as Angola, and they had to cope with Portuguese. Part was designated the Congo – present day Zaïre – and they had to cope with French. Part was designated Zambia and they had to cope with English. And such divisions of Africa have had long-reaching results, and Rwanda today is part of that story.

Philip Kazhila was a Lunda. He came from a family of Jehovah's Witnesses, but left that group behind and came into the membership of one of the denominations that formed, eventually, the United Church of Zambia. He came into the ministry of our Church, and I served with him in the Copperbelt of Zambia. He was a man full of gentle wisdom, and of strong faith, greatly respected, much loved. So much so that we elected him President of the whole Church, and that meant he moved from the Copperbelt to Lusaka.

While he was in Lusaka he contracted cancer. Zambian and expatriate doctors, with all the training and the skill and the medical understanding of western medicine, treated him. They treated him with surgery, with radiotheraphy, with chemotherapy. To no avail.

At that time there was quite a large Chinese population in Zambia. They were building the railway that became the lifeline for the export of copper away from the South, because the borders were closed, towards the coast on the Indian Ocean and Dar es Salaam. They had brought with them a group of Chinese doctors, with their particular expertise and skill in acupuncture. Philip travelled 150 miles north from his home, and went and was treated by Chinese doctors. And to no avail.

And, because in Zambia there were many different forms of faith, there were also many people who offered their specialist ministry of faith healing. Philip went to them. And to no avail. Finally, he went to the man that you and I might call the witch doctor.

Have I ever told you that I lived in the city of Kitwe, the hub of the Copperbelt, an industrial city of 300,000 people? There was a witch doctor in our township. He had a whacking great Mercedes with a blue flashing light on the top! He considered himself to be a part of the medical team, and, of course, he was, because in African traditional medicine there is a great fund of knowledge about the medicines to be derived from trees and plants and traditional methods. But there was also a lot that was suspect, and I, as a white expatriate, was never allowed into that area. I wondered about this highly exalted President of the whole Church going along to a witch doctor. And the old superstitions lie not far below the surface, and die hard. Remember please that we're talking about Africa, still only just over 100 years since white people first went and, so called 'discovered' it, and added their level of civilization. I know that in my congregation, and in others, people wore charms. That as well as Christian baptism there were all sorts of much darker ceremonies conducted around a newborn baby. And old superstitions do die hard, and remain close under the surface.

Can I tell you about David Cruise? David Cruise is a Methodist minister. He's currently Superintendent at the West London Mission. He operates from the base of the church in Hinde Street, but he has inherited all the work, all the social outreach that was developed earlier this century by Donald Soper, and by his forebears. David and I have been close friends for more than 20 years because David, too, served in Zambia, and we were close geographically as well as in other areas. We have much in common, including the fact that Sue, David's wife, like Carol, was redheaded and died of cancer earlier this year.

Perhaps you know that Methodist ministers, when they move, move in preparation for 1st of September, ready to begin the new year. August is a month for moving from manses. David was telling me that some time ago he needed to move in London because he was moving appointments from one part to another. He rang up a number of different removal firms and tried to book a date in August to move. Time after time he was met with a blank wall. No dates available. Until, eventually, he found one removal firm who said to him 'Sorry Guv – completely full, no chance.' That was the end of the conversation; except that it was picked up again: 'I don't suppose you would even begin to consider moving on Friday 13th of August would you? You see, everybody wants to move, but nobody wants to move on that day, it's considered bad luck to go into a new home on Friday the 13th. Of course we'll give you a special discount...' David grabbed it. And the old superstitions run just beneath the surface, and die hard.

Isn't it easy for us here in Chandler's Ford to stand back, to stand aloof, to stand in suspicion and look at those things? Until you remember that when you go round some of the streets of Chandler's Ford there's a missing number in the sequence of some streets and some homes. You have to look hard to find a '13' house. And old superstitions die hard, and remain just below the surface. But, but...

This year we, as a church, amidst all else that has happened to us, all the suffering and all the heartache, have had the triple blow; the death from cancer of Jocelyn, Marj and Carol. Much shock. Many tears. A great deal of heartache and searching questions. Honestly, haven't we asked, and I say 'we' because I'm part of it, haven't we asked 'Why? Why this church? Why us?' And haven't we, in all honesty asked 'What's happening? What's God doing with us?' And deeper, but with that same honesty, can we admit – hardly to articulate it, but admit that it's there – that we wonder about the run of so called 'bad luck', or even about such things as 'jinx'? And don't we know, from these last weeks, that old superstitions run close beneath the surface, and die hard? And in the midst of us being hard pressed, with raw, grieving people, as well as personally and with those families intimately concerned. I believe that part of my responsibility, part of my commitment is to hear, and to be aware of the questioning that is in your heart and your mind, and try with you to struggle, and to find the solid truth on which we as a church are founded.

A month ago I tried to speak about faith in the living God, and faith in the resurrection of the dead, and faith in love that is eternal. I want this morning, in different aspects, to try and answer some of the questions that still persist, and to do so using words, phrases, ideas, faith, from Psalm 103.

> The Lord is merciful and loving, slow to become angry and
> full of constant love. He does not punish us as we deserve
> or repay us according to our sins and wrongs.
> [Psalm 103:8-10 GNB]

Can I pick up two truths from those phrases? 'He does not punish us or repay us.' One of the most important people in all the history of the Christian Church has been Martin Luther. It is important that we remember that we are people of the Reformation, and that the Reformation needs constantly to be rediscovered in our midst. I believe that it is very easy for each one of us slip back into what I call 'balance sheet' Christianity. Balance sheet. Oh, people know at a deep level the reality of conflict between good and evil. Know in their own life the power of sin, and their need of forgiveness and of the mercy of

God. We throw ourselves at God's feet, knowing that we have no other hope. And yet, and yet, so easily we slip into the way of thinking that – well, if we just do enough good deeds, and if they outweigh the bad ones then the balance sheet comes out in our favour, and that somehow we'll slip into heaven. That salvation is all to do with merit, and not God's grace and his mercy.

Martin Luther was important in the history of the Church, because at a very low point in the Church's life people needed to be reminded of that in a very forceful way. People had gone so far down the track of balance-sheet Christianity that they'd started selling what were called 'indulgences', sort of tickets to heaven. You could buy them. You could buy your way in. And Martin Luther said 'No way', and rediscovered all the mercy and grace of God flowing into us. It was a significant moment when the penny dropped again, and he said 'You can't do it.'

In contrast to the pure, holy God who demands perfection, we are worthless, without a hope. Luther held in his hand the amazing truth of the love of God for people like us. Martin Luther said, in effect, God puts his finger on the scales and that the balance is in our favour, and that finger is a person – Jesus. Jesus himself, remember, had to face all this welter of questioning about the root of illness, and the consequence. I read just that snippet from the ninth chapter of John's Gospel [vv. 1-5]. John, as ever, introduces a factual story and goes on at a much deeper level. But there in the mind of the disciples, not the bystanders, the disciples, was the question: 'Whose fault?' Was it the man or his parents? Why is he blind? And Jesus says 'it's nothing to do with sin'.

Now please, for a moment, do not imagine that I'm standing here and saying sin is not important. Please do not, for a moment, imagine that I'm sitting light to sin. Do not, for a moment, believe that I'm offering what Bonhoeffer, a German theologian who was caught up in the plot to kill Hitler fifty years ago this week, called 'cheap grace'. That isn't the offer. It is the costly grace that we proclaim. The cross is the cost. Do not believe, for a moment, that I'm bypassing God's call, God's demand for moral living on Christian people, individual, personal morality, as well as community and national morality. He demands it. He remains pure. He says 'Be perfect'. But we start from nothing, and we end up with nothing, and we need God's mercy and God's grace, and it's that that tips the balance. And it's Jesus. And the Scriptures say:

He does not punish us as we deserve or repay us according
to our sins and wrongs.

Then the second truth, that I want to pick from these verses, is the
truth that the Lord is merciful and loving, even-handed with no
distinction, and (as the Acts of the Apostles put it) has 'no favourites'.
Part of that collection of the sayings of Jesus that we today call the
Sermon on the Mount includes the command that we love even our
enemies as ourselves, and in setting that out Jesus points to the truth
that the sun shines on good and bad alike, that the rain comes to all.
There are no demarcation lines. You can't 'spot the difference'. And
God's blessings shower upon us all. That's the way he meant it to be.

Earlier this year a well-known British symphony orchestra went
abroad on tour to some of the major cities of Europe. Within the
community of the orchestra and its musicians there was a group of
Christians and they, apparently, met together regularly. Sadly, one of
that group of Christians had an accident, falling down a flight of
stairs, and in the course of the accident actually falling on her
instrument, damaging both it and her knee – badly, painfully. Now
that was bad enough, but the worst thing was that that young
Christian – young in terms of young in the faith – said 'Why has this
happened to me?' She said 'Why me? I am a Christian.' You see, not
only do we indulge in balance sheet Christianity, if we're not careful
we indulge in 'insurance policy' Christianity, as if linking ourselves
with God somehow gives us a bypass to the reality of life.

And if nobody's twigged until this morning – it doesn't, and it
won't. We need to take into account mortality that is built in and
inescapable. This is not the moment for any philosophical discussion
about the alternatives in God's creation. This is the way he intended
it. This is the way we are. That isn't to be callous or indifferent, to be
hard-hearted or anything else. It's to recognize the reality of our
human life, and our situation.

When people come to me to talk about the wedding service that is
about to happen within their family, they come, usually, with a sort of
stock list of hymns. Sadly, that list is diminishing as hymns in our
schools are being squeezed out. But one of the familiar ones, one of
the favourites, one of the well-known ones 'Praise my soul, the King
of heaven' is so familiar that I just wonder sometimes, as with other
things, whether we as the Christian community don't read it; we sing

it, and never take notice of the words. If you actually look at the inscription at the bottom of the hymn, you'll find that that hymn is based on Psalm 103. From what we've read this morning together, and from what I've said, do the words 'Slow to chide, and swift to bless' ring bells? Here they are. And here God is. Blessings poured richly on us, and on all the world. But it's more than that as well. At heart, Christianity is about our God, who not only knows about our heartache, and about all the deep questions that begin with 'Why?', but also shares them. And shares them from the inside, from a human life. From Jesus.

Psalm 103, remember, is Old Testament – good as it is – but we as Christian people need to turn on to the New; and need to hear Jesus, and see Jesus, and know Jesus. Surely, amongst the most poignant moments that we read about is that time when Jesus found that his friend was dead. We are told, in the most succinct phrase of the whole of Scripture, that Jesus wept. Then on, even from there. On to the hill outside the walls of Jerusalem and on to that symbol of death and degradation – the cross. On to that moment of sharing, and that moment of knowing, and that moment even of death for God. And because of that death we, today, here, with our questions, can be sure 'the Lord is merciful and loving'.

I have a sequence of photographs at home. I'll gladly show them to anyone who asks! They're of Mount Kilimanjaro, and from a unique viewpoint, taken out of the window of an aeroplane on a journey. We'd landed at the small, relatively new, airport near the Tanzanian town of Arusha – under the lee of that great mountain. While we were on the tarmac, being refuelled, a tropical storm swept across, and the rain hammered down, and the clouds not only obscured the mountain, but enveloped us all. It was some time before we were allowed to take off, and still the cloud covered the mountain. The plane took off, punched through, and came above. And above the storm, and above the cloud, there was the topmost dome of that great peak of Africa – solid and reliable.

And through the storm, and through the cloud, to come through and see solid and reliable still – our God, who is loving and merciful to you, forever. Amen.

Nicodemus Came By Night

Sermon preached by Philip Ward at All Saints parish church, Clifton, Bristol, on 24 October 1993.

Mr Ward, married with three children, has a degree in Applied Physics from City University. He worked for 10 years on The Advanced Gas Cooled Reactor at Sellafield, before seeking ordination. 'I enjoy preaching. It is important because it is a question of trying to communicate the Gospel. If we don't give preaching a role we are failing to communicate.'

Bible text: John 3:1

> One of the Pharisees, named Nicodemus, a member of the Jewish Council...came to Jesus by night.
>
> [NEB]

It was a warm wind. A wind full of the smell of aloes and cooking pots, and ass's dung and wood smoke and people. A warm strong wind, shouldering its way up the streets between the glimmering white buildings, flickering the lanterns, sending the shadows dancing and twirling, blundering up the alleyways with the steep cobbles. Carrying with it snatches of a baby's cry, of laughter, a man's shout, the chuckle of a chicken coop, and soft lovers' noises. Blundering bumptious west wind. Warm wet brat of a wind. Snatching the skirts of the cloak between the legs, tugging the hood from the secret clutching fingers; dignity billowing away like a flag. Hustling, bustling and nudging through the dark mysteries of passage-ways and courtyards.

Careful up the steps so as not to trip. Knock on the door. In. Heave it shut and slide the wooden bolts home to keep out the wind.

'Come in Nicodemus, come in.'

It's so peaceful inside after the wind.

'Take your cloak off, Nicodemus'

The lamp flame burns still and the shadows are soft.

'Sit down, Nicodemus.'

It's quiet in here, it's quiet and peaceful and still.

'Well?'

Well what *have* you come to ask him, respected member of the Council that you are? What have you come to ask him, privately, secretly, by night? You can't just sit. Silence is too dangerous. People get to know each other by being silent. You've got to say something. You've got to hide behind words, otherwise he'll sit there in silence all night and he'll *know* you.

'Rabbi, we know that you are a teacher sent by God; no one could perform these signs of yours unless God were with him.'

There. Does he know how much that cost me to say? There's several of us, even in the Sanhedrin who would admit privately that he is a teacher from God, but today in Jerusalem even the walls have ears. But there's no one here except us. Him and me and the wind outside.

I wish he'd answer, I wish he'd say something. I've given him the opening, haven't I? I wish he wouldn't just sit there like that as if I hadn't spoken, or as if I had said something quite different...What's that he's saying?

'Unless... Unless a man... Unless a man has been born over again he cannot see the Kingdom of God!'

What's this talk of birth? Death is the only thing I've got to look forward to with my arthritic knees and my balding head. 'Born again!' This is religious jargon: meaningless words. In my imagination I can hear countless preachers mouthing them uncomprehendingly. 'Born again!'

'Rabbi. How is it possible for a man to be born when he is old? Can he enter his mother's womb a second time and be born?'

I at least will get a straight answer from him!

'Nicodemus, Nicodemus. O Nicodemus how obtuse you are. No one can enter the Kingdom of God without being born from water and the spirit: no one can enter the Kingdom of God without letting the spirit take them and lift them and sweep them away. It has nothing to do with your part-worn, middle-aged carcass Nicodemus. Nothing to do

*with your myopeia and your tummy. That's flesh. Flesh can only give
birth to flesh, it's spirit I'm talking about. It's spirit. Just listen to that
wind, listen to it. That's what the spirit is like. You're safe in here
from the wind. Sheltered. But being born again is like going out into
it, letting the spirit take you and carry you where it wants, that's what
it's like. Listen to it Nicodemus!'*

I wish that wretched wind would stop: even the lantern is flickering
now. These young men, they want to change everything all at once, as
if God worked that way. Discipline and order, that's God's pattern:
discipline in the faith, knowledge of the law; it's sheer anarchy that he
is teaching, it seems to me, anarchy...

'Lord, how is this possible?'

*'You, a famous teacher of Israel and you don't understand? Don't
you see, I am talking about things I know, things I've seen: but you
won't believe, you won't let go of your preconceptions. You think you
know what heaven is like and how God works, and it is no good me
talking to you because you won't listen to me. Not even about
ordinary everyday things you won't listen, let alone heavenly things.
No one knows what heaven is like except the Son of Man whose home
it is, and he is the only one who knows the way there. But you won't
listen will you? None of you'll listen. You wait for death as if death
were the way. Law and order, judgement and death – and you'll try to
send the Son of Man that way too. You'll lift him up on a cross
Nicodemus. You'll lift him up on the symbol of death. You worship
death, all of you. Do you know what? You remember the story about
the serpents in the wilderness who bit the Israelites so that they died,
and you remember what Moses did? How he put a brass one on a pole
so that anyone who had been bitten and who looked on it could live?
Well that's what you will do. You'll put the Son of Man on a pole:
you'll make him a symbol of death. But anyone who looks at him will
live.'*

It's quiet again in the little room; the lamp flame flickers, then
burns steadily. There's light in here where we sit. There's light,
there's too much light, he can see my face. There's too much light and
it's too quiet. People get to know each other in the quiet. I daren't let
him know me and I'm scared to know him...

Where's my cloak? Wrap it round. Pull up the hood. Hold it close.
A muttered word: *'Mustn't take up any more of your time.'* Then into
the shadows by the door. A deep breath. Draw back the bolts and
stagger back under the force of the wind.

135

Head down. Down the steps. Down into the alleys and streets, down into the dark, secret city, down into the world. Down into the wind. What did he say about the wind? 'Being born again is like going out into the wind, letting the wind take you and carry you where it will.' Hold on tight Nicodemus, hold on, the world is full of the noise and the scent and the bustle of the wind. Hold tight, for you never know where it might blow you!

What Kind of Christian Are You?

Sermon preached by Jim Rea at the East Belfast Mission on 3 January 1993.

The East Belfast Mission is a lively congregation and reaches out to the unemployed, the homeless and people with addiction problems. Mr Rea, awarded an MBE in the 1995 Birthday Honours List, has worked as a Methodist minister in Cregagh in Belfast and Irvinestown, Co. Fermanagh since being ordained at the age of 28. He received a call to the ministry at 18 but needed a job to finance his studies for the ministry, and worked for some years in the clothing and steel industries. A committed evangelical, his main interest is counselling people with alcohol addiction. He gained a Master of Theology from Westminster College, Oxford, on the nature of alcohol addiction and the relationship between religious experience and recovery. On preaching, he says: 'It remains a major means by which or through which God speaks to people. It is not the only way, but one of the major means. Despite the changing styles of communication, and preachers need to take account of this, it is significant that throughout history preaching has remained an important means of communication.'

Bible text: Philippians 1:2-4

> To all the saints in Christ Jesus who are at Philippi...I thank my God every time I remember you. In all my prayers for all of you, I always pray with joy because of your partnership in the gospel from the first day until now.
>
> [NIV]

I remember it well. I was collecting at one of those awful flag days in Lisburn for our Mission. Having rattled my tin box ineffectively I thought I'd try the shopkeepers. So far all that was memorable was the cold day, until I went into a jeweller's shop. The owner looked at me dressed in my clerical attire and then asked a strange question, at least I thought it strange. 'Are you a Christian?' he said. Having assured him that I was, he went on to ask: 'Yes, but what kind of Christian are you?' My answer must have met his expectations for he gave me a pound followed by a loud 'Amen'.

What kind of Christian are you? That question has lived with me for a while. Some of us may, like my jeweller friend, have a fairly fixed idea as to what the answer should be.

I couldn't help but think of a text in the letter of Paul to the Philippians, which gives an insight into the kind of Christians we should really be, and it isn't a narrow definition. It is almost hidden in the first few verses of this little letter of Paul, from prison in Rome to Christians eight hundred miles away, whom he wants to encourage and thank for their concern. The question doesn't directly arise but the answer is there if we look for it. In fact there are four thoughts that come through in Paul's opening remarks that must be a challenge to all of us.

'To all the saints in Christ Jesus,' says Paul. Now there's a thought: 'in Christ Jesus'. That means being *related to Jesus Christ*. Throughout Paul's letters this term crops up: 'in Christ'. It is so often a term used to describe Paul's religious experience that James S. Stewart, the famous Scottish preacher, entitles his book on Paul *A Man in Christ*. It is all about a relationship that involves Jesus Christ living within us, that is, his Spirit living in us.

I remember as a boy watching my hero, goalkeeper Harry Gregg, playing for Manchester United. When I was playing for our street team I thought I was Harry Gregg. But after one match when I had let in twelve goals, my friends assured me that I wasn't. I couldn't be anybody else. Yet the secret of the Christian message is that Jesus Christ can live inside a person. The living power of a personal God can live in us.

That's what happened to Paul on the road to Damascus. He encountered Jesus. Some call this Christian conversion. It is the moment 'when the penny drops'. In his autobiography *Surprised by Joy* (Collins, 1965), C. S. Lewis, after what appears a rather ordinary experience on a visit to Whipsnade Zoo, describes his new experience in this way: 'When we set out, I did not believe that Jesus Christ is the son of God and when we reached the zoo I did.'

It does seem that what makes you a Christian in the New Testament is to have a relationship with God via Jesus Christ. We then become his sons and daughters. As the Gospel writer John suggests: 'Because we believe in him we are the children of God.' In fact, Paul makes a remarkable statement in his letter to the Romans when he says: 'The power that raised Jesus Christ now lives in you.' Resurrection power, the living Christ inside. No wonder the well-known writer Herbert Butterfield can say: 'Hold to Christ and for the rest, be totally uncommitted.' [L. D. Weatherhead, *The Christian Agnostic*, Hodder & Stoughton, 1967]

But there is something else for these Christians that Paul infers and that is that to be Christian means to be *related to each other*. These Christians really did work together. Look at what Paul says: 'I thank God every time I remember you...I always pray with joy because of your partnership in the gospel...' This is important for us today. How well do we work together? A friend of mine whose church at Belvoir Park, Belfast, was blown up by terrorists, was asked by a journalist: 'And how's your church?' To which he replied: 'My Church is fine, it's the building that's the problem.' That said something profound about beleaguered Christians in south-east Belfast. Despite their loss of building they were working together.

The church at Philippi had three members who are known to us. We read about them in Acts. There was a jailor, a fortune-teller and a well-to-do business woman. Different cultures, I guess, but working together.

However, Christians working together in love and commitment is not always how it is. Someone has said that the modern Church has too many 'don'ters, won'ters, can'ters and quiters'. A friend of mine was working with young people at a Yorkshire village Methodist chapel. This congregation had resulted in the coming together of two Methodist congregations, one Wesleyan the other Primitive. My friend hadn't enough coffee cups for the youth group and had been told that there weren't any more cups. However he looked in a cupboard to see dozens of cups. 'But you can't use those,' a lady said, 'they are Wesleyan cups.'

I wonder how well we work together and relate to each other. Remember what Jesus said: 'This is the way others will know you are my disciples that you love one another.' But do we really, are we interested in doing it our way, and doing our own thing, or are we really partners in the Gospel as Paul says?

But there is something else. They were *also related to the community*. They lived at Philippi. Now in the first century that wasn't a bad place to live. It was the most important city in the region. Situated on a high road between Europe and Asia, it was strategically placed for trade. It had a few gold and silver mines. It was also a Roman Colony and this provided some advantages for citizens in the ancient world.

Whatever the situation, Paul describes them as Christians at Philippi. Not all Christians are good at relating to the world. Many people in inner-city east Belfast make the comment about the Church: 'They are not our kind of people and they don't speak our language.'

While the New Testament writers urge Christians in some ways to be unworldly, in the sense in which the opening verse of Romans 12 is translated by the scholar J. B. Phillips [*New Testament from Twenty-Six Translations*, Michigan: Zondervan Publishing, 1966], 'Don't let the world crush you into its mould', they nevertheless urge us to be world-related. We are to understand the people around us and be able to relate the faith to where they are. Looking at Christians leaving their churches after morning service in east Belfast was for me an interesting observation. How different was their dress to those people standing around the streets. Is there not a gap here that needs to be bridged, if we are to relate to our community?

Do we take seriously the words of the children's song, 'Everybody ought to know who Jesus is'? Too often we can become like golf clubs for private members only. I am not sure we always really care enough, although some do. When I visited America a few years ago I came across a young man from Ireland lecturing in a university. After introducing himself, he informed me that he was a committed Christian. However, he went on to explain with a little embarrassment that he had come from a background that was supportive of the IRA. 'However, life has changed for me now,' he said. 'Just after coming to live in the States I got hurt jogging. I went to a physiotherapist to have treatment. While he was treating my leg he was telling me about his faith in Jesus. As a result of meeting with him I became a Christian.' Full marks to the physio.

A friend of mine who died recently was a wonderful Sunday school teacher and Bible class leader in our local Methodist church. One day a friend of mine met him in a newsagent's buying a specialized motorcycle magazine. 'You're not into motor cycles,' he remarked to Robbie. 'No, but I have a lad in my Bible class who thinks about nothing else but motor bikes and I want to get into his world' was the reply.

And that's the task for all of us: to be concerned about our community. That's why Christians in Northern Ireland have got involved in efforts for peace. That's why some have risked their reputations to talk to the IRA and the Ulster Volunteer Force because the Gospel must be related to the community and to those marginalized from the Church. We are to be Christians at Philippi and that means our street and our patch.

However, there is one more thing to consider. Paul didn't call them Christians, he called them 'saints'. A rather holy word. The preacher Leonard Griffith is right when he says in his book *This is Living* [Lutterworth Press, 1966], 'The word saint is a good word gone wrong.' It is more associated with stained-glass windows than real people. In the original Greek of the New Testament it means 'holy', which is another word that needs to be taken out and dusted. 'Holy' means to be set aside for a special purpose and that's what Christians really are, they are *related to a life of Christian holiness*. We are not to be set apart to some remote desert island to keep us from evil, but we are sent out specially for the service of Jesus Christ. If salvation is something God does for us and discipleship is something God does through us, then holiness in something God does in us. This is a real possibility, God can be at work in our lives making us better people. That's why I like the caption that reads 'Please be patient, God hasn't finished with me.'

When I look at one of my friends who suffered from a serious alcohol problem, but who now serves Christ working with other alcoholics, loving them, caring for them, counselling them, I say to myself, 'That woman's a saint.' But not because of herself, as she would rightly admit, but because Jesus Christ is working within her. The words of the hymn writer Harriet Auber (1770-1862) come to mind.

> And every virtue we possess
> And every conquest won
> And every thought of holiness
> Are His alone.

How do we become saints? It seems to me that there are no short-cuts. It is by being committed to Jesus Christ completely. It requires that we develop our knowledge of him by prayer, by Scripture reading, and by worship and service. Some Christians will find the Lord's Supper also important in this regard.

A little girl would pass a parish church with a stained-glass window on which there were the Gospel writers. The window was beautifully backlit with a spotlight. One day in school the teacher asked: 'What is a saint?' Immediately the little girl replied: 'Miss, a saint is someone through whom the light shines.' And that is what we can be and should be, even though we would never like to claim it. For saints are not people in stained-glass windows but people who are and who want to do God's will in God's way, by God's power.

So what kind of Christian are you? Indeed what kind of Christian am I? Are we *related to Jesus Christ*? Not just some kind of formal allegiance to a creed, but a living relationship with Jesus Christ?

Add to that what it means to be *related to each other*. Do we really work together in the Church, putting aside selfish concerns for the benefit of Christ's Kingdom?

Are we *related to the community*? How interested are we in the problems of those in our community? Do we love people because we want to see them converted or do we want them converted because we love them? There's a subtle difference. Are we really trying to understand the language of secular and marginalized people?

Are we *related to Christian holiness*? Being saints and all of that. Well, we really can be. God wants us to be attractive Christians through whom his light shines.

I'm not sure the jeweller in Lisburn, when he asked me that question, ever realized that his question would become a starter for a sermon. I'm not sure how pleased he was with my answer. But then he wouldn't want to be the judge. I guess somebody more important, who can give help with the living of it, wants to know *what kind of Christians we are*.

The Widow's Mite

Sermon preached by Gill Dascombe at Wood Lanes Methodist Church, Adlington, on 2 July 1994.

Gill, 44, married with two children, is also employed as a lay worker in the neighbouring circuit in Macclesfield. The sermon went down so well with the 16 women present that she preached it a second time in Macclesfield, for Social Responsibility Sunday in November last year. Gill, a part-time locum pharmacist and accredited as a Local Preacher in 1987, preaches about 12 times every three months. Gill says: 'What I set out to do is to try and make the Gospel real to people so they can encounter Christ and make their response. I quite often preach, as here, with story preaching. I try to make it come alive and vivid so people can feel as if they are actually there and taking part in what is going on. I find this works as a technique and I get good feedback, particularly from women.'

Bible text: Luke 21:1-4

> Jesus looked round and saw rich men dropping their gifts in the temple treasury, and he also saw a very poor widow dropping in two little copper coins. He said, 'I tell you that this poor widow put in more than all the others. For the others offered their gifts from what they had to spare of their riches; but she, poor as she is, gave all she had to live on.
>
> [GNB]

What is the aim of our faith? To change the whole world, or to change our own hearts? A short while ago, two things happened to me which challenged me deeply. Today I have combined them into a story which I have called the modern parable of the widow's mite. It doesn't give you all the answers, but it may well set you thinking. It certainly did me.

How small the coin looked, lying there in the palm of her hand! She stared at it for a long time, thoughtfully and secretively, as if recalling some deeply personal memories, or thinking out a difficult problem. Finally she turned it over a few more times with her large, dirty fingers, then let it drop, with a clink, into the plate.

I'd seen her before, that woman. At the supermarket. I'd been heaving my shopping trolley towards my car, struggling across the ruts in the car park surface. My trolley was particularly heavy that day. I always try to get a whole week's shopping in one go, to save me time, and with four healthy humans, a dog, three fish and a budgie in the household, we get through no mean amount every week!

She walked across my path. Or rather slouched across. She was grossly overweight, her legs bare and bloated. Her hair was thin and badly dyed; sparse grey wisps emerged from her scalp, blackened ends flapped about her shoulders. Her lipsticked mouth held a cigarette which she had newly lit from another which she had just finished. And she was dirty, so dirty. Layers of ill-fitting clothing, and a pair of grimy ancient slippers on her feet. She pulled a rickety shopping bag on wheels behind her, its contents one or two tins of food, a bottle of cheap gin, and two packets of cigarettes.

And here she was, a couple of weeks later – in church! I felt embarrassed to see her. My first reaction was to turn my head away in disgust. What a degraded, debased example of humanity! What a precious gift is life, and how desperately do some people abuse it! And I thought of the God we were gathered to worship, the loving heartbeat of the universe, who made us humans in his own image to be his delight and his glory.

His glory! *This woman?*

I wondered what had brought her into church today, and suspected her of being drunk. I hoped she would not disturb the service in any way. She shuffled in, dragging the shopping bag behind her, and took a seat near the back. Few people noticed her, and most of those that did see her, pretended they hadn't. The smell was quite pungent.

We began by praising God for the beauty of the earth, and while the children stayed in the service we said prayers of thanks for good homes, loving families, food and health. For my sermon I expounded on some of the theories of the atonement, and then rounded off by talking about the cross as a symbol of coming together, and of reaching out in Christ. To finish we sang Charles Wesley's great hymn:

Come sinners to the gospel feast,
Let every one be Jesus guest,
You need not one be left behind,
For God has bidden all mankind.

At the end of the service, guilt and a sense of duty made me go up and speak to her. A few of the others joined me. What should I say?

'Hello, it's good to see you. Er – awful weather we've been having!'

'Yes, it's cold and wet on the streets. I'm homeless, you see. Nowhere to go.'

I felt embarrassed, inadequate and suspicious. Alarm bells began to sound in my head about gullible do-gooders being conned.

Glad of the chance to escape, someone sped off to the coffee lounge, where the church family were meeting in fellowship, to get her a cup of tea. Equally glad, I shot off to the vestry to see if the Church Stewards could spare her something from the church benevolent fund. But they were too busy counting the collection to come straight away, and when they were free, she had already gone. A few people had seen her off, advising her to contact Social Services the next day.

We stood for a while discussing the situation.

'There's no need for anyone these days to be begging.'

'You often get these people coming round churches, spinning a yarn, playing on our soft-heartedness.'

'She probably didn't even come in to worship, just to get warm. She'll probably spend the money on drink.'

As we turned to go, I remembered having watched her as the collection plate had been going round. I saw her dig deep into the pockets of her grubby mac, and rummage for a long time before she found what she was looking for. I saw her drop in one pound coin, and then hesitate, for long enough to cause a ripple of irritation from the other end of the pew. Finally, the cheap make-up on her eyes smudged as she rapidly wiped a tear with her torn sleeve, before letting the second pound coin fall, slowly and deliberately, into the plate.

Two small coins. All she had to live on.

The plate passed on along the line, but, still suspicious, I kept my eyes on her for a little longer. What happened next was unexpected and incredible. Transformation! She sighed and smiled, and, for a brief second, she was beautiful.

> Jesus looked at his disciples and said, 'Happy are you poor; the Kingdom of God is yours!...But how terrible for you who are rich...
>
> [Luke 6:20, 24a]

I think back to that day with shame at my arrogance. What made me think I was such a shining example of the pinnacle of creation? Me with my tidy life, my smart clothes, my cheque book and my car! Me with my prejudice, self-absorption, self-justification, insecurities, halfheartedness, hostilities, and pathetic attempts at love? What made me think that my clever words would be a more acceptable act of worship than her small, sacrificial, generous offering? What a good thing it is that God is not fooled by outward appearance!

We walked back to our cars, and someone made a final comment. 'These people come for what they can get, then move on. We won't see her again. She won't come back for more.'

They were quite right. She didn't.

The Gate and the Gulf

Sermon preached by Barry Overend at St Chad's Church, Far
Headingly, Leeds, on 27 September 1992.

Barry is married with four children and has been a clergyman for 23
years. He was ordained at the age of 23 after a theology degree at
King's College, London. He has a regular slot on BBC Radio Leeds'
Sunday Breakfast Show, *and his scripts have twice been turned into*
books with the proceeds going to the BBC Children in Need Appeal.
He is also a contributor to the Saturday Sermon *in the* Yorkshire Post
and has done BBC Radio 2's Night Time Pause for Thought. *He says*
'I have always approached preaching as something intended to be a
stimulus for thought rather than as something which is a complete
package or an end in itself. It is important that clarity of message
comes across. A sermon is quite succesful if at the end people can say
what it was about!'.

Bible text: Luke 16:19-31

Let's remind ourselves of the script before we attempt to turn the
story into a film. A rich man – anonymous. A poor man – but
lucky enough to have a name – Lazarus. Some dogs – number, size
and breeds unknown. The rich man dies. The poor man dies. Causes
of death unknown, and totally irrelevant. The poor man in heaven
with no problems. The rich man in Hades with no prospects. Guest
appearance by Abraham. And that's about it.

There you have what I think the film makers call the 'story board'.
Ok, it'll never be a blockbuster. But in the right hands it could be a
cut above a soap.

So supposing it's in *your* hands. Imagine that you're one of those
movie moguls in Hollywood. There you are, sitting in one of those
canvas chairs with your name blazened across the back of it, cigar in
mouth and a sun shield over your eyes. I can never understand why

film producers have to wear those things. Perhaps it's because they're dazzled by their own brilliance.

Anyway, your task is to make a movie of that 'Rich Man–Poor Man' story. I'll suggest a better title for it later on. Now we haven't got time to shoot the whole film in one sermon. But let's at least try to get it off to a good start. For like the first paragraph of a novel, the opening shot of a film is crucial. So what's it going to be?

Well, let's consider the possibilities. You could, of course, shoot it straight. Just lift it from the page and put it on the silver screen. And there's your first shot – the rich man dressed in purple and fine linen, and feasting magnificently. The costume and the food shouldn't present any problem. Your only dilemma is casting. Is the rich man going to be lean and handsome – say Mel Gibson or Tom Cruise – or are you going to have any old actor padded out to look grotesquely fat? After all, this man pigs himself every day.

The set should take care of itself. Something grand and lavish. You could probably pick up something suitable and cheap from the ill-fated *Eldorado* series.

Or maybe you'd prefer to cut the sumptuous scene and go straight in with the shocking: a close-up, perhaps, of one of Lazarus's festering sores, and the dog drooling over it. Your problem there is the dog. You'd need to get that right. I mean, it wouldn't be any good having a little Westie. The audience would all go 'Aah, isn't he sweet! But who's that horrid little man sticking his filthy foot into the dog's mouth?' *Points of View* would be inundated by protests from animal lovers everywhere. And you would have blown the whole thing. So definitely not a Westie, or even a Labrador. No, it would have to be a Rottweiler, wouldn't it? Something which is going to make you recoil in fear just by appearing on the scene, even before it lays a slobbery tongue on poor old Lazarus. That would make a good, chilling start.

But personally I wouldn't go for either the sumptuous or the shocking beginning. For that all-important opening shot I'd focus on the ordinary, but evocative. So my film of this story would open with a close-up of the gate. 'Which gate?' Precisely. The gate on which the story hinges, but which everybody misses. For all the attention it receives, Jesus might as well not have mentioned it. But it's there in the story. It's the rich man's gate. And the poor man lay outside it.

So, what's a gate? No, it's not a trick question. But just think about it for a moment. A gate is a point of entry and exit. It's for coming and going. So it's not impenetrable. It's not a drawbridge or a barricade. But it does, nonetheless, serve as a divide. It marks a boundary. It separates people. And in this particular story it separates a rich man from a poor man. And, most important of all, it doesn't open. It could. But it doesn't. Yet all too often people misread this story as if it did.

The story-line doesn't say that Lazarus was fed by the scraps which fell from the rich man's table. That would have been disgraceful enough. It actually says that he *longed* to be fed in that way. And I take that to mean that he wasn't. The dustbin wasn't put out for him to pick through. *Nothing* ever came through that gate to benefit Lazarus. That's just the way it was – in this life.

End of scene one. Intermission, adverts and ice-creams! Now back in my movie-mogul seat I have to shoot the scene in the next life. Shall I open up with the splendours of heaven, or focus on the torments of Hades? Or maybe I should go for the personal angle and bring in 'Father Abraham' right at the beginning of this scene. A guest appearance by Howard Keel perhaps. No, none of that. I'm going for the gulf, the 'great gulf'. For that serves the same purpose in scene two as the gate in scene one. It's the separator, the divider, the boundary mark between the rich man and the poor man. But, unlike the gate which doesn't open, the gulf doesn't close.

So when the rich man requests – or is it demands – that Lazarus be sent over to cool his tongue, Abraham doesn't say: 'How dare you! You've got a nerve!' He just says: 'It can't be done. The gap is unbridgeable.' Nowhere in this story does Abraham, or Lazarus for that matter, censure the rich man. The story merely states facts. It doesn't moralize. And the facts are pretty simple. Once upon a time there was a rich man and a poor man separated by a gate. Now upon a time there's a rich man and a poor man separated by a gulf. Only the rich man is now the 'poor' man, and the poor man is now the 'rich' man.

But there's another striking difference now that we've come back to the film 'after the break', as they say. All of a sudden the formerly rich man desperately wants to make contact with the formerly poor man. Oh, the irony! And we weren't supposed to miss it, surely. In scene one, all the rich man had to do was to stroll down his garden, lift the latch, and it's: 'Hello Lazarus, is that your dog? Come on in!' Or at least: 'Would you like some left-overs?' But that's precisely what never happened. Now it's too damned late. And in the context of the story, 'damned' is the right word. The rich man, who chose to live in splendid seclusion, is now damned to hellish isolation. The gate which could have opened has become the gulf which can't close. That's why I'd call my film of this story *The Gate and the Gulf*.

For there's the rub of the story. It's about the divide between people. And that's what I'd want my film to focus on. And the gate and the gulf would be the appropriate images. But I wouldn't want my film hi-jacked by well-intentioned people, keen to turn it into an advert for Oxfam or Christian Aid. There's so much more to the story than just a message about giving to charity, or helping those who are worse off than yourself.

Granted, in this particular case, it was wealth and poverty which divided the two men. But it could have been religion, or race, or politics, or education, or class, or a hundred and one other things.

Here then is a story which prompts us to open up – perhaps our pockets, but more likely our hearts and minds, to the people whom we choose to shut out. And to do it before the gap between us becomes unbridgeable. That, after all, was the whole thrust of Jesus' ministry – to invite those who'd been kept at bay: the diseased, the tax-gatherers, the sinners, even the women and children. If, in contrast to Jesus' attitude, we insist on keeping ourselves to ourselves, we may eventually be left to ourselves, and that might prove to be more hellish than we've bargained for. It's a self-centred existence which I once heard described as 'keeping yourself in perpetual safe-deposit where you don't accrue any interest and become less and less interesting every day'. Perhaps the real reason why selfish people aren't allowed into heaven is not because they're particularly sinful, but because they're just too plain boring to have around the place for evermore. So, like sulky adolescents, they're told to take their miserable selves off.

But I don't think this story about the Rich Man and the Poor Man, or as I prefer to think of it, the Gate and the Gulf, was ever intended to give us detailed information about the next life. Who knows what happens there? And frankly, the idea of finding myself in the bosom of Abraham somehow just doesn't appeal. I'd certainly cut that from the film version. Well, let's be honest, if you've got to have a bosom in your movie, you wouldn't go for Abraham's, would you? And I don't think I'd bother with the flames of torment either. I'd just want a shot of that unbridgeable gulf to speak for itself – conveying the dreadful possibility of eternal abandonment.

And then, to finish with, I'd do what Leonardo da Vinci did in his famous painting of the Last Supper: I'd put myself in the picture. There I'd be, looking out across that chasm to the people on the other side – Abraham's side. There'd be a shot of Lazarus sitting at the top table with a whole host of unlikely people. And I'd be asking: 'How on earth (or better, 'How the hell') did they manage to get in?' And a voice would answer: 'They just opened their gate more often than you did...' And then let the credits roll.

Yes, I know I've missed out the tail-end of the story – the bit where the rich man wants Abraham to send Lazarus on a mercy-mission to his five brothers. And that in turn leads into Abraham's comment about people not taking any notice even if someone went to them from the dead. A comment which, of course, is meant to make us think of someone else who hasn't actually featured in our film as yet. But look, these days any film which is worth its budget will run to a sequel. So I'm keeping those bits of the story for *The Gate and the Gulf 2*.

In the meantime, there's no denying that – like a child opening the door to a stranger – it's a risky business opening your gate to every Tom, Dick and Lazarus who's lying outside it. Taking yourself off safe-deposit certainly means that you start accruing interest, but it also involves the terrible possibility of losing everything you'd been trying to preserve. The French priest, Michel Quoist, recognized the danger and wrote about it in one of his *Prayers of Life*:

> Lord, I was so peaceful at home, I was so comfortably settled. It was well furnished, and I felt cozy. I was alone, I was at peace. Now, Lord, I am lost! Outside people were lying in wait for me. I did not know they were so near; in this house; in this street; in this office; my neighbour; my colleague; my friend.
>
> As soon as I started to open up I saw them, with outstretched hands, burning eyes, longing hearts, like beggars on church steps.
>
> The first ones came in, Lord. There was after all some space in my heart. I welcomed them. Till then it was sensible. But the next ones, Lord, I had not seen them; they were hidden behind the first ones. They come bending under heavy loads; loads of injustice, of resentment and hate, of suffering and sin. They drag the world behind them, with everything rusted, twisted, or badly adjusted. I can't stand it any more! It's too much! It's no kind of a

life! What about my job? My family? My peace? My
liberty? And me? Lord, I have lost everything, I don't
belong to myself any longer; there's no room for me at
home.

Well, if that is what happens when you lift the latch, is it any
wonder that the rich man kept his gate firmly shut? For if you once
open it, there's no way of knowing just who may gate-crash into your
life. 'Precisely!' says the ending of Michel Quoist's prayer:

Dont worry, God says, you have gained all. While others
came in to you, I, your Father, I, your God, slipped in
among them.

So, for God's sake, let's leave our gate ajar!

The Pearl of Great Price

Sermon preached by Edmund Marshall at Howden Methodist Church, Humberside, on Sunday 19 March 1995.

Dr Marshall, 55, who gained a doctorate in pure mathematics from Liverpool University, lectures in management science at Bradford University. Dr Marshall, married with one daughter, has been a local preacher of the Methodist Church since 1959 and has also been licensed as a Reader in the Church of England since October 1994. He attends and preaches in churches of both denominations regularly. Dr Marshall has published two books, including Parliament and the Public *(Macmillan, 1982) and* Business and Society *(Routledge, 1993). He says: 'Preaching is conveying God's message to people everywhere and, as such, it is one of the most significant activities that anyone can be called upon to undertake. I am constantly amazed as a preacher how often God uses me to say things which are more meaningful to the listeners than I could have ever imagined.'*

Bible text: Matthew 13:45-6

> Again, the kingdom of heaven is like this. A merchant looking out for fine pearls found one of very special value, so he went and sold everything he had and bought it.
>
> [REB]

Unlike most precious jewels, pearls are not mineral in origin, but are the products of living creatures. Gems may be from the mountain, but pearls are from the ocean. There they are found in the shells of oysters, molluscs and other shellfish, particularly in the warmer waters of the Mediterranean and Red Seas, the Persian Gulf and the Indian Ocean. Because they occur in that part of the world, pearls were very well known to peoples of ancient history, who regarded them as jewels of prime value. The Roman writer, Pliny the Elder, described pearls as 'the most sovereign commodity in the whole world'.

Precious possessions of any kind were often compared with pearls. Jesus, for one, makes such comparisons. He tells his followers not to cast the pearls of Christian truth before swine, where they will be trodden underfoot in the dirt. And in making one of his metaphorical descriptions of the value of the Kingdom of heaven, again a pearl comes to his mind, a pearl of very special value, one for which the merchant is ready to liquidate all his stock and possessions and invest his whole fortune. The Kingdom of heaven is truly the most valuable experience, the priceless experience, for any human being, so valuable that we have to be ready to forego and sacrifice everything else to attain it.

But Jesus is not alone in the New Testament in comparing heaven with a pearl of great price. If you turn to the Book of Revelation you find St John there describing the twelve gates of the new Jerusalem as twelve pearls, every single gate being one enormous pearl. No one can enter heaven except through one of those pearls. As we sing in one of our hymns:

> Through gates of pearl streams in the countless host,
> Singing to Father, Son and Holy Ghost, Alleluia!

The city may be of pure gold, the walls of jasper, but the gates, the vital ways in, are massive pearls. The entrance to eternal life for every one of us is through a pearl.

Now if pearls are found in the shells of oysters, how do they come to be there? Biologists tell us that pearls are created as a result of damage suffered by the oyster or other shellfish. If the shell of the oyster is broken, either by accident or by some tiny, boring parasite and if grains of sand or some marine worm penetrate into the interior of the shell then the natural reaction of the oyster is to exude a powerful liquid secretion to plug the gap or imprison the foreign body. This secreted matter rapidly solidifies to become a pearl. While the inside walls of many shells may be coated with the shiny material which we call 'mother of pearl', it is only when there has been damage done to the shellfish that a proper pearl in globular form is to be found.

In this way, it is to survive and to defend itself against attack that the oyster forms one of the world's precious gems. Pearls are the product of damage and suffering. Oysters which lead normal, quiet lives produce no pearls. They are of value only for human consumption. But the oyster which suffers produces a pearl of longstanding value, and the deeper the suffering, the larger the pearl. In the gem trade, the largest pearls are known as paragons, and it is the paragon which is created by the worst damage to the oyster.

For us it may seem a far cry from the scene that we normally associate with pearls, the glittering sparkle of a necklace of pearls in the elegance of some stately ballroom, to the wretched suffering of small shellfish at the bottom of the sea. But there is a direct connection. Without the damage endured by shellfish, the necks of wealthy women could never be adorned by pearls. Pearls demonstrate the inextricable link between suffering and real wealth.

But the pearls which make up the gates of heaven have not been formed by the suffering of any shellfish. These eternal pearls of great price are created by the eternal suffering of Christ. He is our oyster, opening up for us the world of eternal life by the precious pearls made of his infinite agony on the Cross. It is by the penetration of the nails through his hands and by the piercing of his side with a spear that spontaneously there exudes forth the fullness of God's eternal love to form the perfect beauty of the paragon pearls which are the gateways to heaven for every man and woman. It is by the nails and spear of Calvary that we can know the riches of eternal life, the boundless love and grace of paradise. The central message of the Christian faith is that Christ, by his limitation in material flesh, his rejection by human beings, by his crucifixion and resurrection, has opened the door to eternity, the door which is the great pearl of his love, the pearl of great price, which, for each one of us, like the merchant of the parable, is worth more than all other possessions and interests put together.

In this way. the natural suffering of the oyster, repelling invaders in the dark depths of the tropical ocean and creating the pearls that adorn the rich, symbolizes for us all the vicarious suffering of Christ, hung on his cross and building the entrances to the Kingdom of heaven. Eternal achievement is born out of eternal suffering.

So too, in minor form, with our own experience. As soon as we are committed to following Christ, then we have our own crosses to take up, and we should not be surprised when they bring us real suffering. They would not be crosses otherwise. Sometimes they will bring suffering of a physical nature, because of our material frailty or propensity to disease and exhaustion. Sometimes they will bring mental agony and torment because of the awkwardness of human nature, within ourselves as in others. Sometimes our crosses will bring intense frustration and depression over the state of the world and life around us. However great may seem such suffering to us, we should not resent that it happens to us as Christians. And we have always to remember that our pain is small when compared with the universal agony of Christ over the world.

At the same time we have to realize that, through our suffering, God may be calling us to make some pearl for him. It is often only through suffering that real goodness can be achieved in this life. No new baby is born without at least some pain and discomfort for its mother, sometimes very great pain and danger. So too, if we look at most of our painful experiences, we shall see them pregnant with pearls. It is not just sentiment that enables us to see most clouds with silver linings. There is something in the nature of human experience that, where there is no suffering, there can be no striving for real improvements in human affairs. It is out of pain and distress that concentrated effort arises to find a better way of life. Advances in medical research have often been inspired by the agony of a sickbed or a tragic death. Many road improvements come about after a spate of accidents with mutilated motorists and pedestrians. As Dr Sangster used to say, lighthouses were all built by drowned sailors.

So, whenever we experience suffering, the question we have to try to answer is what is God calling us to achieve through this pain. What pearl does he want us to help to create out of our tribulation for the benefit of all people? All human suffering has to be seen as a challenge to reduce and overcome its incidence, to form pearls of permanent value for the human race. There will be many circumstances when, because of our Christian commitment we have to be ready to face and endure suffering, ready to assume heavy burdens, in order to attain results of real and lasting value.

In the Old Testament, the story of Job is a monument to worldly endurance and physical travail. Job knew what it was to suffer. In many ways his story foreshadows the coming of Christ into the world, a deliberate act by God to endure tribulation, temptation and self-sacrifice in order to secure the reconciliation of the world with himself. He is always at hand to share our suffering. We have to face opportunities of being crucified with him in order to achieve something of good in his sight.

If we spend our lives trying to avoid all suffering, discomfort and great effort – and in the modern western world such aims are attainable for some people – then our achievement will be very superficial, soon forgotten, lost when our bodies perish. But if we want to make pearls, we have to accept pain. We must dive deep into the ocean of life to find real pearls. As John Dryden wrote in one of his poems:

> Errors, like straws, upon the surface flow;
> He who would search for pearls must dive below.

Unless our lives are to become useless flotsam, tossed around inconsequentially on the surface of events, then we need to launch into the deep, to accept the likelihood of pain and suffering, and follow Christ in making and discovering pearls that open up the road to heaven.

And when we do discover such pearls, everything else has ruthlessly to be put aside so that we can concentrate entirely on the development and growth of those pearls. Like the merchant in the story, we have to concentrate all our resources, energies and abilities on building up the pearls for the benefit of all people. Then we shall be sharing a little of the experience of Christ on his cross. We shall be sharing in his production of pearls which are the gates of heaven, and in fellowship with Christ we shall be taken through those gates to live with God for evermore. Amen.